WHEN WORDS GET IN THE WAY

a journey with aphasia

Elaine Schultz &
Kevin E. Hadduck

When Words Get In the Way: A Journey With Aphasia
Copyright © 2022 Elaine Schultz & Kevin E. Hadduck

Produced and printed by Stillwater River Publications. All rights reserved. Written and produced in the United States of America. This book may not be reproduced or sold in any form without the expressed, written permission of the authors and publisher.

Visit our website at
www.StillwaterPress.com
for more information.

First Stillwater River Publications Edition

ISBN: 978-1-958217-35-1

Library of Congress Control Number: 2022912636

1 2 3 4 5 6 7 8 9 10
Written by Elaine Schultz & Kevin E. Hadduck.
Cover & interior book design by Matthew St. Jean.
Published by Stillwater River Publications,
Pawtucket, RI, USA.

Names: Schultz, Elaine (Elaine Allison), author. | Hadduck, Kevin E., author.
Title: When words get in the way : a journey with aphasia / Elaine Schultz & Kevin E. Hadduck.
Description: First Stillwater River Publications edition. | Pawtucket, RI, USA : Stillwater River Publications, [2022]
Identifiers: ISBN: 978-1-958217-35-1 | LCCN: 2022912636
Subjects: LCSH: Schultz, Elaine (Elaine Allison) | Aphasic persons--Biography. | Aphasic persons-- Family relationships. | Aphasia. | Parents of children with disabilities. | Parent and child. | LCGFT: Autobiographies.
Classification: LCC: RC425 .S38 2022 | DDC: 616.85520092--dc23

The views and opinions expressed in this book are solely those of the authors and do not necessarily reflect the views and opinions of the publisher.

I want to thank my mom for always believing in me, my dad for his support, and Kevin Hadduck, without whom this book would not have been possible.

I must say a special thank you to Anna, my younger sister, who was in effect my supportive and encouraging big sister through much of our childhood together. Thank you also to the teachers, doctors, therapists, tutors and friends who have worked alongside me throughout the years.

I dedicate this book to the memory of my grandparents, Arlene and Bob Smith, who did so much to help me discover myself.

Contents

Foreword		*vii*
Introduction		*x*
1	Oh the Things We Say	1
2	Birth of a Question Mark	6
3	Adoption	12
4	When Words Get in the Way	16
5	Elaine, the Law, and Us	22
6	Comfort, Complexity, Vulnerability	33
7	Ready, Reset, Stop	42
8	A Sharp Downturn	46
9	New School, Old Troubles	54
10	A Deepening Crisis	68
11	A Legal Fight Takes Shape	78
12	Expectations, Claims, Realities	91
13	Pedagogies at Issue	102
14	Summer Ends In Exhaustion	111
15	A Year Begins…to Crumble	116
16	IE…Procrastination	123
17	Crash	129
18	A Bright Direction	136
19	Toward a Stronger Self	140
20	A Steady Walk	152
Epilogue from Elaine		155

Foreword

When I first met Elaine, we shared stories of our experiences at Carroll College, my alma mater and the college she currently attends. Elaine explained her frustration as she watched her fellow students struggle to advocate for themselves. She shook her head as she described how she wanted to teach them to navigate the accommodation process and self-advocate. At the time, Elaine spent much of her time advocating in some capacity: for herself as she requested accommodations for college classes, and also for her aging family members as they navigated the complex insurance and healthcare systems. Elaine's mom, Barb, explained that this had not always been Elaine's role. Not that Elaine had been incapable of advocacy, but that she had not always been allowed the opportunity to advocate.

From the time of her birth, Elaine's parents had become her defenders. Like many parents of disabled children, Don and Barb were often forced to defend the very worth and dignity of Elaine's existence, warding off healthcare providers and educators that preferred to see Elaine removed from her family and placed in an institution. Elaine was born before the passage of the Americans with Disabilities Act and almost a decade prior to the landmark Supreme Court Olmstead Decision of 1999, which established the right of disabled people to receive support in their communities and not be segregated in institutions. This decision represented a monumental victory in the effort for deinstitutionalization and was integral to preventing institutions from becoming the default placements for children like Elaine. As Don and Barb insisted that Elaine remain with their family, they did so at a time where systemic discrimination against the disabled community was not only normalized but often promoted.

As Elaine matured, the role of her parents, much like the role of all parents, had to evolve. Barb relayed that it was not until Elaine was a teenager that she realized that her goal could not and should not be to protect Elaine for eternity, but to allow her opportunities to learn how to advocate for herself, to take risks, and to embrace her own agency. She had instilled these values in Elaine throughout her childhood, as she worked to expose her to disabled representation that disrupted the narratives perpetuated by an education system that refused to accommodate her and a healthcare system that maintained that there is one correct way for a person to interact with the world.

In the face of professionals who consistently told Barb what Elaine could not do, she had relentlessly insisted on what her daughter could do, what she was capable of. Now it was time for Barb to embrace the truth of her advocacy, that Elaine was no longer a child in need of protection but a teenager in need of the resources to navigate the world independently. While parents of disabled children are often encouraged to maintain control over their child's life, Barb's insistence on Elaine's worth and potential led her to embrace the natural transition of parenting to recognize that Elaine must be the authority on her own life.

Just as Elaine is the authority on her own experiences, she must also be the authority on the telling of them. This story is a telling of Elaine's life as she perceives it. This is not a consensus published on behalf of the disabled community; this is the telling of one experience. However, while specifics and perceptions may vary, the sentiments of this story are far-reaching. While Elaine began her education twenty-eight years ago, many families today continue to struggle to defend basic rights that have been mandated by federal law for decades. In many cases, this minimum legal requirement has yet to be realized. Speaking with Elaine about the many predictions made about her life, it is hard to comprehend that her family was told that she would never learn. Barb remembers questioning this prediction, asking whether the doctors had a "magic eight ball." Throughout this story, it is apparent that it was not Elaine's aphasia that was limiting but her environment and the stigma towards it. The greatest barriers Elaine experienced were due to a failure to accommodate her. Her learning style did not conform to an arbitrary concept of "normal," and so she was dismissed as unteachable. However, when her family insisted on teaching Elaine in a manner with which she could be successful, she thrived. Far more disabling than Elaine's aphasia were the attitudes she encountered.

Our society has developed around one conception of the human experience. We have designed our systems and environments for people to walk instead of roll, to hear instead of lip-read, and in Elaine's case, to have an auditory learning style instead of a visual one. While Elaine's story is unique, it also shares the common theme of discrimination maintained in the stories of many who exist in the world in a manner that defies the assumptions that have shaped our society. As you read Elaine's story, I urge you to imagine how this story would change if our society was constructed to accommodate and appreciate the diverse ways in which people interact with and exist in the world.

Rachel Bechtel

Introduction

Elaine walked into my disability services office early in the fall of 2015. She hesitated at the door, but came in and sat down, avoiding eye contact and rubbing her fingers together continually as we talked. Handing me some documentation, she explained her disabilities: aphasia and anxiety. We then built an accommodation plan for her time at Carroll College.

For the most part, Elaine looked like other students, albeit a few years older than the traditional freshman. What distinguished her most, however, was her reticent expression, an almost flat affect that suggested more than mere shyness. She spoke with a soft voice, often hesitating between phrases, as if she was not sure exactly how to articulate her thoughts. She sat forward in the chair, not quite facing me, only looking tangentially in my direction.

Nothing about her left me feeling troubled or worried, however. Nothing about her demeanor nor in our conversation led me to believe that she might not succeed at Carroll. Elaine belonged at Carroll College, her aphasia and anxiety notwithstanding. Her full-tuition, presidential academic scholarship made that emphatically clear. In fact, Elaine has done well throughout college. As we write this book, Elaine is moving steadily toward graduation with her peers.

Elaine tells her story here primarily to teach and to encourage, but who needs to learn? Who needs encouragement? Too often, our attempts to formulate answers fall, almost inevitably, into a "we-they" formulation, and thus into misunderstanding. Our inclination is to question *their* capacity for learning and, thus, to grant *them* a condescending encouragement. We do not so easily question ourselves.

Elaine hopes her story will help break down that polarizing and paralyzing formulation at the heart of so many of our troubled conversations. She does not want pity, as if suffering and struggle uniquely define her existence. Nor does she want excessive admiration as another posterchild for those who overcome great obstacles and whose achievements tempt us to wonder why more disabled people do not figure out how to buck up, toughen up, and will away their supposed deficiencies. Elaine does have an important story to tell, nonetheless, and yet a common story about herself and about us.

Elaine recently sat across a small table from me in her home, pausing for a moment to think. She looked at me and said, *"How can I tell, or show, when language is so difficult?"* She chuckled and continued, *"I mean, without tears and yelling! In elementary school, I needed something like sign language and body language."* It may have been in third grade that Elaine first so concisely and poignantly summed up her difficulties: *"Words get in the way,"* she said. Now, at thirty-one, Elaine speaks fluently when relaxed, comprehends very well, and recalls with only moderate difficulty. She communicates with a keen wit and a ready sense of humor about her life as a person with disabilities or "differences." Our labels get in the way too.

Very early in her childhood, Elaine became aware of her differences and often expressed to her parents and teachers, *"I can't talk because other people don't understand."* At home, Elaine's aphasia manifested in her relationship with her sister. She and Anna loved playing together, but they also fought, as siblings do. Many of their squabbles, however, stemmed from Elaine's inability to speak clearly. She remembers saying to her mother Barb, *"I've been telling Anna so fast,"* or *"I've been trying to tell her so hard, but she doesn't understand."*

Don and Barb, Elaine's parents, describe Elaine as a "very sensitive" and perfectionist child, who held everything in and worried a lot—most deeply about losing a loved one or a pet, but also about her ability to learn, to keep pace with her peers, and to fit in socially. While she quickly picked up on other people's emotions, she struggled to express her own. As a result of those difficulties, she has met occasional abuse, frequent resistance and, most often, simple misunderstanding throughout her school years.

Such challenges have occurred less frequently over the years; many school administrators and teachers have by now accumulated a great deal of formal training and experiential knowledge regarding the requirements laid out by the Individuals with Disabilities Education Act (IDEA) and the Americans with Disabilities Act (ADA). Improvements on college campuses have often followed student activism and the faithful work of ADA coordinators and disability support providers.

Nonetheless, updated laws, training and experience among professionals, and increased student awareness have not eliminated the problem of discrimination. Elaine will still encounter the thoughtless professor or student who blurts out some frustration or impatience. Of her travails through a long group project in one college course, for example, she says, *The other students always rejected my ideas. I felt awkward. They didn't get me. They treated me like I was stupid. The professor was nice, and I tried to explain what was going on in the group, but she didn't really understand either.*

Elaine's most difficult and sometimes humiliating experiences involved her own frustrations with understanding, processing, and producing words. Those same experiences, however, inevitably involved other people assuming an incapacity on her part, and thus not listening carefully, deliberately enough truly to *hear* her.

In fact, Elaine knows that she knows; given adequate time and mental and emotional space, she can prove it. Elaine has done well throughout her education, both in her childhood years and now as a college student. Her success has come at the cost of grief served up by others and of her own extraordinary effort, a process of relentless review, rethinking, revision, and recalculation.

Elaine's aphasia targets the language centers of her brain; most educational processes likewise target those language centers. If Elaine's experience is somewhat unique, it is precisely because her specific learning difficulties pose an almost comprehensive challenge to the heavily verbal teaching methods that most teachers use.* For Elaine, words often get in the way.

In a society that so highly values self-sufficiency, industriousness, and hard work, Elaine has acquitted herself magnificently. Our hyper-valuation of self-sufficiency, on the other hand, has meant for Elaine varying degrees of ostracism and neglect, as someone with disabilities who needs help that others often seem reluctant or ill-equipped to give.

She asks for help, despite her anxiety, but she also has taught herself to learn independently. She employs study techniques that she has learned from others and discovered for herself. For instance, she borrows video tutorials but also creates her own, which other students have found helpful. While learning college calculus (and earning an A for the course), she used video tutorials, whiteboards, diagrams, drawings, and phone pictures of her own work. She made a practice of solving multiple preliminary problems in order to solve one for an assignment. Her processes are slow at times, of necessity, but effective.

As we write this book, Elaine continues her college coursework, majoring in computer science and engineering, with a substantial load of math. "*Math is ok,*" she says. "*It is concrete, factual, discrete, even if complex. Words are so ambiguous, and they have emotional content.*"

Through years of learning to learn as a person with aphasia, Elaine has become a creative and empowered student. Faithful advocacy and guidance from her parents and teachers has served her well, but so has her own initiative, persistence, and creative thinking.

---

* *The use of "visual learner" and "visual learning" in this book is not meant to place the education of Elaine within the debate about the validity of "learning styles" theory and the teaching methods that derive from it. Instead, it seems reasonable to assume that Elaine's aphasia places her mostly beyond the parameters of that debate. She does learn from reading and from verbal instruction and continues to work very hard at improving her verbal learning skills. Nonetheless, her specific disability presents remarkable challenges to her facility with language. I will address this briefly elsewhere in the book.*

We tell this story now, nearly thirty years after the passage of the ADA and forty-five years after passage of the IDEA. In the years since the passing of those key legislations, parents, schools, and courts have continued to wrestle and wrangle with the law, refining policies and practices as the struggle for equal opportunity continues. We preserve our legislative victories for civil rights, only through a continuation of the battles.

Early in the drafting process, Elaine and I sat in my home talking about this book. We talked a lot about "voice." Whose voice will tell Elaine's story? *"It's been a little strange hearing my mom read the book out loud so far. I don't think of myself in the third person. I will begin reading it myself soon and let you know if anything you have written needs to change,"* she said of it.

Indeed, this is Elaine's story, and it is her voice that we want readers to hear. My role is to help her tell of her own battles, defeats, and victories, from her beginnings to her present place in the world.

CHAPTER 1

Oh the Things We Say

*Sticks and stones may break my bones . . .
but words may break my heart.*

A Kindergarten Trauma

In August of 1993, Barb and Don enrolled Elaine in kindergarten at the elementary school in Belleville, Illinois. Elaine remembers that most children in her kindergarten class seemed comfortable around her and communicated with her well enough by adapting to her differences. Some, inevitably, keyed on her inability to communicate well verbally. Noticing her indistinct and sometimes garbled speech, they occasionally teased her. She had also developed an embarrassing left-side drool, as her mild cerebral palsy manifested in a slight drooping of her face. Despite that, it was her fellow students who most often provided her with a sense of security and belonging.

One incident of bullying, early in first grade at Belleville, might actually have begun with a word spoken several months before by her kindergarten teacher, Tanya Albay. Both that word in kindergarten and the incident in first grade remain vivid in Elaine's memory.

One time at lunch in first grade kids started teasing me. I don't know what started it at that moment, but it started with one kid and had a sort of ripple effect. Kids started calling me a retard. My speech was so bad at that time. I couldn't hardly speak a sentence at that stage. They didn't know how to deal with someone who could see and hear, but not speak.

Elaine had learned the meaning of that word, "retard," in kindergarten, and hearing it again was painful. *"You don't forget such things,"* she says.

Indeed, teasing from her first-grade classmates that day called up her memory of a devastating experience from her kindergarten class. With her enrollment in the Bellville elementary school, Elaine discovered that kids were not, in fact, the source of her deepest stresses. *"It was mostly the adults I had trouble with,"* she says now, *"especially my teachers."*

Mrs. Albay maintained a "very fast and very verbal" teaching style. Elaine could not understand verbal instructions easily in any case, and the teacher's speed of delivery compounded the problem. Likewise, Elaine could not communicate her frustrations effectively, and her parents reported that she "held it all in" each day, even at home.

The teacher's written responses to Elaine were consistently negative. Barb recalls Elaine often coming home with a "sad face" that her teacher had drawn on her completed in-class assignments. Elaine, Don, and Barb all found the little drawings disheartening; Barb and Don also found the absence of helpful comments or suggestions to be both frustrating and insulting. Elaine's teacher seemed unable to respond comfortably or competently to a child who could not readily understand her or communicate easily with her. Elaine describes her emotional dilemma: *"I noticed when adults got frustrated with me. I would get frustrated, too, because I did not know how to talk the way they wanted me to. I think it was a common issue between adults and me. I think it stressed them out."*

As a result, Elaine suffered almost constant frustration. She recalls not wanting to be in school at all and, thus, not paying attention consistently. "I think that was half the problem," she will say now, self-deprecatingly, with an ironic smile.

As Elaine and I sat in her living room, talking about these early memories from school, one kindergarten class session stood out. She did not tell the story with any apparent bitterness and even blamed herself somewhat for exacerbating the situation. But the story still calls up tears. *"It was a bad day, and I think it could have gone more smoothly. I think I pushed the teacher over the edge. I don't know why. She didn't know how to handle me. I wasn't listening to instructions. That is what tipped her. I liked coloring…"*

Elaine stopped the story briefly and took a few deep breaths. *"I don't have fond memories of school in Illinois,"* she said next, and chuckled softly.

The teacher had grown frustrated with Elaine's seeming inability or unwillingness to follow her verbal instructions. She had directed the students to use the correct colors when coloring a picture of an apple, but Elaine chose a set of colors more to her own taste. When the teacher noticed Elaine's failure to comply, she grew visibly agitated, snatched Elaine's picture from her, then walked away, muttering to the other students, "She's just retarded."

Elaine heard the teacher's remark and the students' laughter, and although she did not then know what the harsh word meant, she felt uneasy. After class, she asked a friendly janitor for the meaning. Knowing nothing of the circumstances, the janitor gave Elaine a simple, straightforward answer. "It means someone who is not smart," he said. In fact, Elaine is both highly intelligent and highly capable. In any case, that old term, long considered harsh and insulting, had no rightful place in Elaine's classroom.

Elaine's kindergarten teacher, Tanya Albay, did apologize a few years later after having a special-needs child of her own. While that apology has helped Elaine through the healing process, the old humiliation still stings deeply. We let our words slip out so easily, so thoughtlessly.

Words Hurt or Heal, Hinder or Empower

Throughout the decades following passage of the IDEA and ADA, professionals in the educational, medical, and legal communities have conducted a necessary and, at times, intense debate about words, specifically about the labels we apply to people with disabilities. The words "disability" and "disabled," central to the law and to professional discourse, have provoked many years of debate over appropriateness, both of denotation and of connotation. If we declare a machine disabled, for example, we generally mean that it no longer functions. We set it aside for repair or replacement. We might otherwise refer to that machine as "broken down" or "done." We clearly mean quite other things when we use the term in reference to a human being, and thus the label "disabled" can be not only insensitive but entirely inaccurate.

Yet we struggle to find appropriate, alternative terms that express respectful sensitivity toward people with disabilities. Some object to the word "disability," while others have reclaimed it as appropriately and matter-of-factly descriptive. In any case, it pays to distinguish between uses of "disability" (or "a disability") and of "disabled." One may experience a disability; one is not therefore "disabled" and may, in fact, be supremely able. The same sort of distinction in usage can apply to the words "impairment" and "impaired."

Some prefer to use the phrase "differently abled," as properly highlighting someone's abilities rather than disabilities. For instance, people with dyslexia often display extraordinary abilities (with spatial recognition, for instance). Still others believe that the phrase "differently abled" does not adequately accommodate the great diversity of physical, intellectual, neurological, and emotional issues covered under the IDEA and ADA.

Another controversial term, "suffer," will make a limited appearance here. Professionals generally eschew the term, as it too often elicits an unwanted pity or creates a counterproductive sense of melodrama. Elaine does not want pity. On the one hand, she has suffered, at times acutely. Thus, suffering plays an integral role in her life. We want a language that gives a full human expression to our realities. On the other hand, Elaine will not tolerate pity or condescension. She was and is tough, and intentionally so. From her earliest years in school, she has very much wanted to be and has been as independent as possible.

In this story, I defer to Elaine's preferences; it is, after all, her story. Elaine prefers a respectful yet duly matter-of-fact language that does not set her apart. The constant wrangling over language can itself feel like a search for euphemism, the language of avoidance, shame, or pity, as if people with disabilities are hyper-sensitive and thus need protection by (and from) the rest of us. To some ears, the well-intentioned results of the debate, conducted primarily among academicians and activists, can sound clinical or ideologically stilted. Such language counterproductively sets "them"—people with disabilities—apart. Finding the right words in context, with the right connotations and nuances, grows complicated.

The debates continue. In the end, we want words that do not get in the way of understanding, of providing needed assistance, or of showing simple respect. We want humane words that empower. For people with aphasia, for whom words pose unique challenges, that search for the right words grows especially poignant and personal, perhaps articulated best as a simple plea: Talk to me, more than about me.

CHAPTER 2

Birth of a Question Mark

What words define, describe, and empower Elaine? From her birth forward, the problematic nature of language and of storytelling bore a central importance for Elaine. What is her story? Who gets to choose the words of her narrative?

Every birth comes with uncertainties, of course, but uncertainty defines every aspect of Elaine's emergence into the world. Consider a newborn about the size of a small cottontail rabbit, or two twenty ounce bottles of water, or perhaps six sticks of butter. Her birth doctor noted that "Elaine was born at twenty-seven to twenty-nine weeks gestational age...weighing two pounds nine ounces." An average birth brings a baby about three times that weight.

Moreover, the diminutive size of a preemie often indicates more than a simple lack of time in the womb for development through an otherwise normal progress. A premature birth can result from, yet also result in, complications that require extraordinary urgent medical care.

A Question of Survival

Born at Mesa General Hospital in Phoenix, Arizona on July 4, 1988, Elaine was X-rayed, then transferred immediately to St. Joseph's Hospital in Phoenix. In his report, under the heading of "Overall Assessment," the attending physician, Dr. Hart, marked the box for "Questionable." Following a series of ultra-sound scans, Hart then laid out a long list of concerns for Elaine's heart, lungs, and brain. His notes, interspersed with technical language, convey a clear sense of urgency: a slightly enlarged heart surrounded by "abnormal densities," bradycardia, "continuous turbulence within the patent ductus arteriosus," apnea, probable hyaline membrane disease resulting from tardive lung development, high bilirubin counts, "probable periventricular leukomalacia" (death of small areas in the brain around fluid-filled ventricles), as well as concern about the presence of "bruising of the head, brow, and right shoulder."

Given the urgency of the multiple birth complications, Dr. Hart kept Elaine in the pediatric ICU for over a month.

While Elaine's overall health indicators were strong at birth, she nonetheless needed immediate attention from a team of doctors and nurses. "There was respiratory distress at birth," noted Hart, "and Elaine required intubation for one week." Hart indicated that he and the nurses also struggled to place the umbilical vein and artery catheters correctly, and Elaine needed a "bag and mask resuscitation with oxygen, followed by intubation."

After a few days, Hart and his team administered the first dose of indomethacin, a non-steroidal anti-inflammatory medication used for treating certain heart disorders. Indomethacin also brings significantly increased risks of bleeding, infection, stroke, heart failure, and long-term complications.

The month of August proved especially harrowing. On August 1, twenty-seven days after her birth, nurses again had to intubate Elaine, then extubate, and then intubate again. Hart made note that day of his ongoing concern over a developmental issue involving blocked nasal passages. By August 3, Elaine had weaned from respirator to room air, but on August 13, Hart recorded possible fluids around or in her lungs. Six days later, Elaine suffered a collapsed lung, a problem that persisted for a full week and would not be resolved fully until August 24.

On August 19, Hart discharged Elaine from neonatal care to the newborn nursery, nonetheless recording his continued concern about her delayed lung development. Virtually every detail of Hart's report indicated the risks and complications attending Elaine's low-birth weight and, thus, the tenuous nature of her existence. She left the hospital with an APNEA monitor for chronic respiratory problems. She needed almost constant attention, especially frequent holding, by Don and Barb and a special nipple for her bottle. Barb took Elaine for many visits to the doctor and many trips to the emergency room at the hospital. Given the nature of Elaine's medical challenges, Don and Barb both felt compelled to learn CPR.

Where Did this Girl Come From?

Elaine's fourteen-year-old birth mother had come to the emergency room of Mesa General Hospital in Phoenix, Arizona, at 12:34 a.m. According to Dr. Hart, she had been in labor for a couple of hours before realizing it. "It wasn't until she began to have some bleeding that she became aware this was a labor process," he wrote. The hospital had no record of blood type and no medical records of any sort regarding the young mother. Dr. Annette McCormick, a clinical neuropsychologist reviewing Elaine's birth history some years later, noted that Elaine had received "no prenatal care" and that, under the stress of a difficult pregnancy, her mother had self-medicated with alcohol, methamphetamine, and marijuana, leading to an uncontrolled vaginal delivery.

Records from the State of Arizona provide only a few details about Elaine's birth parents. Her father, a seventeen-year-old high-school student, enjoyed math and art, a "good student," according to school officials. Her mother, a fourteen-year-old eighth-grade student, also enjoyed math, as well as English.

The only other information from State of Arizona records lays out a family history for both parents that may explain some of Elaine's susceptibility to complications at birth. Both families had histories of heart disease, cancer, diabetes, and hearing or vision problems, among several other issues. On the maternal side, a family medical history included tuberculosis, obesity, and congenital birth defects. Social workers and the paternal grandmother suggested that Elaine's mother suffered from depression, also common in her family history. In response to her pregnancy, her heavy use of drugs may have been a suicide attempt, following news that she could not keep Elaine.

A Question of Identity

In the forty-two days from Elaine's birth to Barb and Don Schultz officially assuming responsibility for her, a picture of profound uncertainty emerged. Who was this 2.6-pound person? Would she live? If she lived, would she thrive? Would she suffer a permanent, severe disability? Her birth mother had given her up; her presumed adoptive parents did not yet have her. What name she was given may or may not remain her name. Her brain, heart, and lungs all suffered some damage and some developmental complications, as if her tiny body had not yet decided to be.

What could be said of her? She was human. She breathed, but she did so only with mechanical assistance at first. Others had decided for her that she would live, but no one had yet celebrated her life. What does an untethered birth mean, when the umbilical cord no longer traces back to anyone? What does a birth mean that looks forward to questions only, to the awaiting identity of strangers who do not themselves know what will come?

Beyond the acknowledgements of her existence, as noted in the technical language of Dr. Hart's hospital reports, perhaps nurses caressed her miniature limbs, cooed to her, and warmed her with their hands. She was blood-type "B-Positive," but blood might never connect her to anyone, past or future. An infant curled in a fetal position takes the form of a question mark, but in a normal birth, parents, family, and society stand waiting with answers. "Her name will be …her mother is…her father is… her siblings, her house, her family heritage.…"

In an adoption placement agreement that Don and Barb Schultz eventually signed, a disclaimer says this: "Catholic Social Services can make no guarantee as to the child's future physical, mental, or emotional development."

Every Question Answers a Story

Elaine's difficulties continued long beyond the weeks immediately following her birth, and those ongoing challenges become key elements of her story.

On the one hand, most of her gross motor delays resolved into normal developmental milestones when her premature birth was factored in. For example, while she did not sit up until nine months or walk until fifteen months from birth, she took her first definitive steps at twelve months from the date at which a normal birth would have occurred. Her mild cerebral palsy and "toe walking" were an exception to that, but eventually she would display significant athletic abilities, despite "minor left-side motor difficulties," according to a pediatric psychologist, that remain to this day.

McCormick notes that, at age eight, Elaine still displayed some extraordinary challenges with fine-motor skills. She struggled with various fasteners and with cutting meat, for instance, but her "excellent eye-hand coordination" made video games easy.

Elaine's most persistent and serious physical challenges were largely due to tardive lung development and infection. According to the Catholic Social Services Family Study, completed in Arizona, Elaine suffered frequent ear infections, wheezing, head colds, and bronchitis throughout her first eighteen months to two years. By the age of five, Elaine had been hospitalized many times, and she continued asthma medications until the age of ten.

On the other hand, Elaine's cognitive difficulties persisted as a consequence of the brain bleeds (strokes) at birth. Through her first few years, she remained generally difficult to handle. She was particularly difficult to feed. She would accept or reject food based upon its texture, for instance, and remained less sociable and "very stubborn and challenging," as Barb recalls, finding it especially difficult to adapt to changes in her routines.

Most of her challenges stemmed from Elaine's frustrations with language. Although highly responsive to visual stimuli, like sign language and pictures, Elaine experienced ongoing, significant speech delays. She "was not a vocal baby," says Barb, and did not say "dada" until ten months old or put two words together until eighteen months. Her speech remained very unclear for some years into her earliest education.

Elaine communicated most successfully, however, by using both oral and visual signals, pointing and grunting, her quick frustration revealing a disparity between her demonstrable understanding and her ability to express clearly what she knew and needed.

Elaine remembers nothing of her own birth and very little of her first three years, of course, but she carries the details of her story like memories. Those details still partially define her, rooting her challenges within some explainable reasons, some unanswerable questions, and some intractable realities. Elaine recalls when she first began learning her own birth history:

I didn't begin learning and understanding much about my own background until nine or ten years old. Before that, I didn't know that Mom and Dad had been working behind the scenes to get me out of the school. I was still learning who I was, learning how the English language worked. I sometimes wish I had understood more of what was going on. Some people, including my parents, told me a few things now and then, but I began to understand only after I started homeschool. Then I was the "deer in the headlights."

As Elaine learned her own story, year by year, she confronted new questions she had not known to ask before.

CHAPTER 3

Adoption

Who Were the Schultzes?

Don and Barb met as undergraduates at the University of Nevada in Las Vegas and married on July 28, 1984. Don's sojourn in graduate school began soon after. Their story bears the elements common to many graduate school couples. Barb remained very supportive of Don's progress through medical school and through his residency in Arizona, sometimes working two jobs in order to meet financial obligations. Don pursued a specialization in pathology, as this career path promised a future of more regular and manageable professional schedules and more time, therefore, with family.

From Arizona, Don and Barb then moved to Illinois, where Don would serve out his obligation to the Air Force before launching his career as an independent professional. Despite the rigors they already faced, Don and Barb wanted to build a family; and for them, that meant adoption. They made a plan.

Adoption Process and Approval

In January of 1987, Barb and Don began researching the possibility of adopting a child. They first contacted Catholic Social Service of Tucson, Arizona (CSSTA) in April of 1987. In May, Don graduated from medical school in Reno, Nevada, and the two moved to Tucson in June. Once they had settled in, they stayed in the same house, a warm and amply spaced home well suited for raising children. CSSTA began their adoptive study of the Schultzes in October and approved them for adoption in January of 1988.

Program specialists and doctors from the Elsa Sells Clinic had sent letters to the CSSTA, affirming the Schultzes as excellent candidates for adopting a child. Don and Barb had not hesitated to accept Elaine, and through all the stresses, "The Schultzes remained positive and patient, never indicating a selfish thought," their CSSTA case worker observed. Two years later, another case-worker report from CSSTA, addressing the Schultzes' application to adopt a second child, provided a compelling portrait of the Schultzes as parents. "I highly recommend Barbara and Don Schultz as excellent adoptive candidates for a second placement," and "Our agency is proud to have Barbara and Don in our rank of adoptive families."

Throughout the adoption study, the case worker noted that the "outstanding quality" of Don and Barb's marriage "is their patience and unselfish attitude." The case worker's highest praises came through her evaluation of Don and Barb's ability to parent, having reviewed their work with Elaine from the previous two years. "It is this worker's opinion," she said, "that Barbara and Don Schultz have displayed exemplary capacity to parent children. I am confident that this is a shared evaluation by my supervisor."

Don and Barb began their adoption of Elaine six weeks after her birth. On August 17, 1988, a case worker with the CSSTA sent a letter to Don and Barb. "This letter will verify that Dr. and Mrs. Don Schultz are approved adoptive parents through our agency," it said, and "The Schultzes assumed responsibility for Elaine Allison on August 16, 1988."

Post Adoption

After Elaine's placement with the Schultzes, Barb worked only at home. The Schultzes' income was low but adequate, as the Air Force paid for Don's final year of medical residency in Tucson. They managed to accumulate a small savings but anticipated a far stronger financial standing as soon as Don could begin his career. Both benefitted from strong family support as well.

Prior to the adoption being finalized, the Schultzes were required to report all serious health issues and any moves to new locations. Throughout that probational period and long after, they monitored Elaine's progress closely, renewed CPR training, held her long and often, and enrolled her in a Newborn High-Risk Program at the Elsa Sells Clinic and in the Arizona Division of Developmental Disabilities and Habilitation Program. They met the unique challenges posed by Elaine's chronic respiratory illness, the frequent visits with doctors for testing, trips to the emergency room, and tending to an APNEA monitor, all while realizing—and at times worrying about—the tenuousness of Elaine's future, and particularly the uncertainties of her future intellectual capacities and physical health.

In those programs for at-risk infants, Elaine benefitted from therapies for "lack of response to auditory stimuli," but tested out of both programs after a little less than a year. The Schultzes also participated often, sometimes as guest speakers, in classes organized by the Catholic adoption agency in support of other adoptive parents and families. The pattern that formed around Don and Barb revealed highly engaged, empathetic, thoughtful, and responsible parents.

Despite the troubling circumstances of her birth, Barb and Don maintained regular (non-revelatory) contact with Elaine's birth parents through the Catholic adoption agency. It struck their case worker as noteworthy that Don and Barb did so, despite their understanding that the mother's prenatal lifestyle might have contributed heavily to Elaine's chronic health issues. They continued sending letters and photos, maintaining a connection that they knew still mattered deeply at the time and that would always matter.

In a letter dated October 6, 1991, Barb and Don conveyed a difficult decision to the birth parents, who had requested a visit with Elaine. The

Schultzes let the young parents know that a meeting with Elaine, now only three years old, would be unwise. Elaine was not yet ready for the answer to a question she could not yet comprehend. The letter displayed a deep empathy on the part of Don and Barb, as well as a carefully and thoroughly considered logic. Recalling a meeting with the birth-father's grandmother, mother, and sister in 1989, Barb wrote, *"We adore your mom and were honored to meet your grandmother and sister...but the question we felt we had to answer was: How would this meeting benefit our daughter?"* They had to think first and last of Elaine's welfare, her inability at three years old to understand what "adoption" meant, and what it would mean for to hear someone say of a stranger, "This is your father." The Schultzes insisted that they would always maintain regular contact with the birth parents, but a meeting between them and Elaine would have to come at Elaine's initiative, when she had matured enough to absorb the realities involved.

Elaine eventually made peace with why her birth parents had left her to be adopted, but that journey took many years.

> *I first learned about my birth parents when I was seven. I didn't want to hear about it. I had no problem with being adopted. My sister and I both knew Don and Barb loved us. At ten, I began to feel like I had been rejected, like my birth parents didn't love me because I was not good enough. I knew that Don and Barb loved me, but I didn't understand why my birth parents let me go. I was about ten when Don and Barb offered to let me meet them. They said Anna could meet her birth parents too. She said yes, but I said, "No way." I was angry, and I stayed angry for a very long time—until my mid-twenties. I felt like my birth parents had just left me to die.*

In the meantime, Don and Barb continued their lives as the parents of a toddler and then of a schoolgirl with profound speech and language delays that they would eventually understand as "aphasia."

CHAPTER 4

When Words Get in the Way

Aphasia

Aphasia results from injury to the brain. Most often, the injuries and the resulting aphasia follow strokes among the elderly, but the condition might otherwise result from trauma to the head, infections, or tumors that damage the language center of the brain. "Aphasia is an impairment of language, affecting the production or comprehension of speech and the ability to read or write" (www.aphasia.org).

The severity of aphasia varies greatly from one individual to the next, leaving some patients almost incapable of verbal and written communication, yet others with only mild and temporary speech, writing, or comprehension impairments. The effects of the brain injury might also remain very specific: a difficulty in remembering the names of objects, for instance, or in constructing sentences or in reading. More often, however, someone with aphasia will face multiple challenges to communication while also nurturing various modes of communication as a means of working around the disability (www.aphasia.org).

Barb Schultz explains an important distinction between those who experience damage later in life and those who, like Elaine, experience damage to their brains at birth. For someone who suffers a brain injury and aphasia after having gained language skills, aphasia means the loss of those skills, while meanings of words and understandings remain. Thus, the essential difficulties involve recall and expression of what someone has already learned.

For the infant, however, no language or meanings have yet been established, so there is no recall to begin with. The initial learning of language, therefore, proceeds in the context of an impairment. An understanding of this distinction between impairment of recall and impairment of initial knowledge formation will become essential for Barb and Don, as they begin Elaine's education. A failure to grasp this distinction, by some of Elaine's key educators and administrators, will inevitably contribute to conflict and frustration for those same professionals, as well as for Elaine.

Elaine's Case, in Brief

At birth, Elaine suffered brain bleeds—or "strokes" as we call them in adults—resulting in damage to the language center of her brain. Testing and observation would eventually establish Elaine's diagnosis as "aphasia," as well as a mild cerebral palsy, resulting in some right-side weakness, slight coordination issues on her right side, and "toe walking." McCormick's psychological evaluation from January of 1997, when Elaine was nine years old, establishes the diagnosis and provides this explanation of the broad term "aphasia:" "a disturbance of any or all the skills, habits, and associations of spoken/written language, produced by injury to certain brain areas which are specialized for these functions."

In a 2006 evaluation of Elaine, a pediatric neurologist, Dr. Cochran, reconfirmed that diagnosis of "moderately impaired" with "global aphasia," including specific manifestations of "non-fluent speech" and difficulties with repetition, comprehension, and naming.

Elaine's earliest symptoms manifested in significant difficulties in both processing and producing spoken language, including some "phonetic paraphasia"—producing words that are phonetically similar to the desired word but different in meaning. For instance, Elaine would say "crunches" instead of "crutches." Her reading comprehension suffered as well, in part because of her weakened verbal comprehension. In fact, among students with language impairments, struggles with verbal comprehension almost always lead to delays in the development of phonetic decoding and thus of reading skills.

From ages two to three, Elaine's speech delays alarmed Don and Barb. Thus, very early on, they looked for help and began monitoring Elaine closely, becoming highly attuned to her emotional patterns and verbal and non-verbal communication habits. They both learned some basic sign language, which they then taught to Elaine. "A great breakthrough," they recall, as the use of sign language expanded the range of Elaine's modes of communication, freeing her somewhat from the immediate frustrations of speaking and listening.

No Real Irony Afterall

To the uninformed who associate "learning disability" with "intellectual disability" or fundamental cognitive impairment, it may seem surprising that Elaine consistently performed well on tests of her cognitive abilities. In fact, Elaine's fundamental cognitive abilities tested within the average or typical range for children her age. According to Dr. McCormick, writing in January of 1997, "Elaine can converse about familiar subjects with help from the listener…and does not have any cognitive delays." Indeed, Elaine tested poorly only when tests were "verbally mediated." Her visual memory ability tested consistently in the superior range, and she struggled with focus and attention only when verbally overstimulated—when too many words, written or verbal, came at too fast a pace.

This disparity between verbal and visual acuity showed up in Elaine's play with other children. She much preferred the less verbal and more physical play typical of boys at that time over the more language-intensive exchanges with girls. Indeed, she rarely initiated conversation or play with other girls, engaging with them less readily and less confidently. As we will see later, Elaine's first serious conflict with a friend, another girl, involved her struggle with clear verbal expression.

Elaine recalls befriending Don's Air Force buddies at four and five years old, often beating them at the video games, Street Fighter 2 and Mortal Combat. Put simply, Elaine repeatedly proved her strong capacity for learning and performing, while struggling specifically with verbal comprehension and expression.

For the sake of understanding disability law and the process of devising appropriate pedagogies and other routine life strategies for students with aphasia (or other language-related disabilities), it serves well to remember that developmental language delays do not in fact mean the same thing as cognitive delays. In other words, Elaine struggled to *express verbally* the full extent of her knowledge and comprehension.

Crisis and Recovery

Understandably, Elaine anticipates social situations with some anxiety, even now. While she generally speaks fluently and comprehends readily, too many words or distractions can lead to a temporary, partial loss of capacity. This regularly posed a challenge in her early childhood, sometimes severe. Throughout her preschool and public elementary school years, for instance, where classroom interactions grew noisy and unpredictable, Elaine experienced what Don and Barb call her "shutdowns." After years of working on computers, Elaine describes her crisis responses as "*a defense mechanism.*" "*I was overwhelmed with everything, like a computer abruptly shutting down, but staying in the process of rebooting and trying to do a self-diagnostic in order to repair itself.*"

As Elaine so eloquently stated in third grade, "*Words got in the way.*"

In fact, a catastrophic "shutdown," deeply frightening for Elaine, Don and Barb, and Elaine's therapist, would eventually precipitate Elaine's move from public school to homeschooling. We will revisit this issue in detail later in the book.

Over time, Elaine's initial symptoms diminished. Her skill at managing her aphasia improved as did her confidence. Such improvements came through the persistent and skillful work of her parents, her sympathetic teachers and therapists, and her own tough-minded determination, even as a very young child.

Although Elaine still struggles with the effects of her aphasia, they are not severe now. Dr. Cochran's evaluation of Elaine in 2006 at age eighteen indicates strong computer and video game skills as well as advanced math and academic problem-solving skills. She advances through college courses in theology, literature, and history. Elaine learns and comprehends complexly.

Elaine continues to face moderate challenges with "executive function": daily organizing and tracking of tasks and mundane problem-solving. She prefers routine. She is "um...not spontaneous," say Don and Barb, with a pause and a smile. Elaine agrees. "*It helps me to follow a plan,*" she says, laughing. "*When we make a plan and then Mom or Dad suddenly change it, I'm like, 'Wait! What are you doing?'*"

Elaine's Language Conundrum

Elaine explains the fundamental conundrum of language as both the vehicle of and yet the obstacle to her communication with others:

> *Between teachers and the many other adults who struggled to understand me, I lacked the skills to communicate or did not know how to communicate clearly through the tone and pronunciation of words. My broken sentences were a barrier. I was desperate and wanted to speak clearly to everyone and not be afraid to speak up.*

She had reason to fear, as speaking up often led to confusion and misunderstanding, and sometimes to abuse.

> *There were times in my life when no one really understood what I meant...misunderstandings of what I meant to convey sometimes made me appear ill-mannered and lazy. The fear of being called*

"retarded" or "dumb" was at the back of my mind all the time, and this only brought out my anger at times, unfortunately.

Elaine remembered her kindergarten and first grade experiences with the insulting word, of course, so she often felt more comfortable, unthreatened, and thus safer among other kids with disabilities. *"This is why I felt more comfortable with deaf people or someone who had a speech disorder or someone who could not speak at all or someone with a learning disability."*

Among such students, words did not get in the way.

CHAPTER 5

Elaine, the Law, and Us

We confront three fundamental issues when working with people who, by medical diagnosis and legal definition, have a disability: 1) what constitutes "normal," 2) what narrative of "disability vs normalcy" we engage with, and 3) how we open the door fully to those whom we have habitually (individually and systemically) excluded from our narratives.

Who Is "Normal"?

As a little girl, Elaine was "*highly aware,*" as she recalls, of her difficulty understanding and being understood by others. These peculiar challenges and differences were then and are now the focus of frustrations. On the one hand, the labels "disabled" and "person with disabilities" trouble her. "*Those labels keep people down, dependent,*" she says. She learned to advocate for herself, insisting that others accept her as "normal."

> *I want people around me who know me to acknowledge that I can function like anyone else can, speak for myself, navigate on my own, whether following directions and instructions or figuring things out myself. I don't want to be labeled as "disabled" or "stupid" or "very dependent on others" in a normal life that all adults must go through.*

Elaine explains, accurately, that she is indeed normal.

I want to be known as a person who can walk, speak, and understand well enough to get by, in spite of my challenges. I do not treat my aphasia as a hindrance, but just a part of me that I have to accept and learn to work around. I may be slow at times, but I'm very capable still to do the work.

Definitions of "normal," however well motivated within a medical or educational community, tend toward the psychologically and medically narrow and the socially and economically convenient. Noteworthy athleticism, for instance, despite being the gift of very few humans, falls comfortably and profitably within our definitions of "normal." We expend vast sums of money and time on athletics for our children, from early childhood through college, straining personal and institutional budgets.

We question the cost-effectiveness of full inclusion for our disabled children, however, as if the athlete provides an obviously robust return on our investments, while the disabled person does not. If we expand our definitions of normal, even if just thinking pragmatically, to include the difficult, challenging, risky, and disabled, we do not pretend that a disability does not present a challenging reality or that appropriate accommodation is not expensive; but we discover that the disabled among us do in fact contribute enormously to our welfare as individuals and as a society.

If we engage the issue more deeply, considering the compassionate and moral and not merely the pragmatic, perhaps we are then more likely to assume without question that attending first to the basic needs of everyone, regardless of condition and cost, is the "normal" and right thing to do.

What Story Do We Tell?

For some, all such stories as Elaine's taken together feed into a pragmatic calculus about the value of a human life and the limits of what the cost of sustaining that life should be.

A young woman with cerebral palsy walks into a Disability Support Service office at a college. An administrator turns to a budget report and begins fussing over the cost of accommodation.

A dyslexic boy takes his seat in a fifth grade classroom. A teacher grumbles to herself that such kids will never be indulged with accommodations in the adult workforce.

A baby girl, born several weeks prematurely, suffers brain bleeds. As the early years pass, and Elaine faces evaluations and reevaluations, both medical and educational professionals respond hastily with unwarranted judgments.

Not long after finalizing the adoption, a neurologist at the University Hospital in Tucson told the Schultzes that "Elaine would not be able to learn. You should place her in an institution." He then asked Don and Barb why a physician's family would want to deal with a child who might never learn.

A doctor at St. Joseph's Hospital suggested that Elaine may never be able to run. Elaine does have mild cerebral palsy and is a "toe walker" (walking on the balls of her feet, without touching her heels to the ground), but a prognosis that felt hasty at the time sounds laughable now.

A few years later, while attempting a Child Find evaluation (a legal obligation to identify and accommodate children with disabilities), a school psychologist became frustrated and said, "She will never learn!"

In each case, the professional begins with an ideological bias or a personal prejudice and reasons outward to the many and remote lives that merely illustrate the "truth" of her or his predetermined point of view. This process often engages the common fallacy of confirmation bias—an illogic that depends upon not seeing human particularities or not attributing full humanity to particular humans.

Every story unfolds as a story within a story within a story, of course; yet we may need to turn the order of concentric narratives inside out in order to see what we most need to see. Seen one way, the conflict that would eventually arise between the Schultzes and the Montana City School District served as just one more example among many of how the

IDEA and ADA met resistance, misunderstanding, and fear in a local and state context.

That set of contexts nestles within the larger national story of how the IDEA and ADA came to be, slowly altered the course of education and labor nationwide, and eventually defined the *intention* of full inclusion for people with disabilities into the educational system and the economy. That perspective places the IDEA and ADA at the center of the story. We see then a grand battle of ideologies, social theories, and political maneuverings. We read of long, arduous courtroom battles for individual rights and institutional responsibilities and legislative contentions over economic costs versus basic human rights. We witness numerous protests and sit-ins, some lasting for weeks, all within the broader civil rights movement.

By that perspective, Elaine serves as just one illustration among millions. That broad national story does and should catch our attention, even catch our breath, if we pay it proper attention and see the fine details of it.

But the glory, to give a twist to a cliché, is in the human details.

Seen another way, in other words, Elaine's story, indeed every individual story, holds center stage. The panorama of national and state legislative battles on behalf of the disability rights legislation serves as context for the considerations and conflicts within a school district and within a school. The deliberations of school boards, administrative committees, and parent-teacher meetings, likewise, provide the settings in which the central narrative unfolds: the story of Elaine. In other words, the narrative that carries an essential meaning for every one of us is the human story at the heart of the broader local, state, and national histories.

In fact, this story begins with Elaine—even before her birth, a birth mother of fourteen, a birth father of seventeen, and Don and Barb Schultz. Barb's response to the doctor at St. Joseph's hospital was quick and passionate, but entirely rational: "And what crystal ball are you looking at?" She added, "You're not God. Your job is to encourage, give hope, and realize that every child has the ability to learn. A child will rise to the bar you set." Stay focused on the child, this child.

Who Opens the Door?

By inverting the order of our concentric narratives, we keep Elaine (and other individuals) at the center of the set of larger stories. In order to see Elaine as ordinary, as "normal" rather than "special," we need to expand our definitions of what ordinary and normal are. When we keep those definitions narrow, conveniently and self-protectively restricted, we excuse ourselves for finding Elaine troubling and burdensome.

We place Elaine outside the boundaries of what we expect of ourselves as parents, teachers, administrators, bosses, coworkers, and legislators. In fact, Elaines are many among us, and she is, after all, immeasurably more like us than not, regardless of whatever measurable differences she may have. More to the point, Elaine is us; we are Elaine.

We allow our false bottom-lines of funding and workload to tell us otherwise. We embrace narrowly in order to serve our convenience or to protect our personal and professional comfort zones. Meanwhile, we spend easily, both time and money, where spending gives us a feeling of empowerment.

In a contemporary culture of "helicopter parents" and "bulldozer parents," questions about intrusion, over-involvement, and over-protectiveness will certainly come to mind among educators reading this story. Such questions can, in medical and educational contexts, carry great significance in determining individual and institutional obligations under the IDEA and ADA. Such questions can also provide a smoke screen behind which some institutions will hide their reluctance to engage with cost- and labor-intensive disabled students.

In the absence of any proactive enforcement mechanism for IDEA or ADA, advocacy by parents, students, and disability support offices most often determines if and how a student is accommodated. As one disability rights activist said to me, "It is very easy to break the law if no one is advocating." We think of "students with disabilities" when we ought to think also of "institutions with disabilities," indeed, of our institutions and society as being dysfunctional and disabling. In other words, we tend to lay a heavy burden of responsibility on the individual but only the lightest burden on ourselves, the institutions, communities, and societies we build. We expect the individual to "overcome" the very obstacles we thoughtlessly place in their way.

If we follow that way of thinking, we remain blind to two sets of realities: First, people with disabilities do not "overcome," as if putting their disabilities behind them in order to function like the rest of us. Instead, they learn to cope, manage, and devise workarounds. Second, the same can be said of almost everyone; we cope, manage, and create our self-specific strategies.

Many of us identify as having a disability. Most of us experience at least one variously disabling condition at some point in our lives and in variously accommodating or resistant socio-political contexts. In so far as we employ the concept of "disability," we must therefore allow that disability exists on a spectrum, the "severity" depending greatly upon our collective responses to it. Thus, "disability" is always, in part, a social construct.

Those of us who seem gifted with a life free of substantial obstacles from birth or imposed by circumstance should not forget that such a life is itself an accident of birth and circumstance (if such a life really exists). We grow comfortable in a world designed by and for us, then wonder why *they* do not fit in. *We* feel tempted to ask, in other words, "Why can't *they* just...?" The answer is quite simple: they can, if we will just get out of their way and, when necessary, make a fair and level way for them.

Let me carry this a bit further and offer a critical view of my own use of the pronouns they, them, and their. There is no definable "them." We are all "us." We set ourselves apart by dubious categories and forget our common humanity.

Individuals with Disabilities Education Act

The laws defining who is disabled are reasonably straightforward for the most part. Defining eligibility for accommodations, on the other hand, poses some daunting challenges to interpret. The greater complexity derives from the fact that no law specifically defines what an accommodation is. The law demands equal opportunity and leaves it to educators to devise appropriate and effective means of achieving equity. Such are the accommodations we invent.

While schools at all levels still struggle to understand and implement the laws clearly and consistently, one can rightly expect a basic understanding on the part of teachers and administrators in 2020. By now, most schools have some programs in place for providing the assistance that students with disabilities need. And by now, teachers, counselors, and administrators have (or certainly should have) a vast reservoir of experience to draw from as they make decisions about curricula, syllabi, lesson plans, and the adjustments to them that we call "accommodations."

When Elaine began school, some of the most influential laws were still new, but the movement toward full inclusion through accommodation had begun much earlier. The Elementary and Secondary Education Act (ESEA) of 1965; the Rehabilitation Act-Section 504 of 1973; the Individuals with Disabilities Education Act (IDEA) of 1975; and finally, the Americans with Disabilities Act (ADA) in 1990, passing just two years after Elaine's birth, had stirred up both hope and resistance among teachers and administrators in private and public schools, from elementary through university levels.

The IDEA states an essential as well as beautiful truth about the place of disability, and therefore of people with disabilities, in our society:

> Disability is a natural part of the human experience and in no way diminishes the right of individuals to participate in or contribute to society. Improving educational results for children with disabilities is an essential element of our national policy of ensuring equality of opportunity, full participation, independent living, and economic self-sufficiency for individuals with disabilities. (https://sites.ed.gov/idea/about-idea/access 03/05/2020)

Here the language is straightforward, at least up to the phrase, "ensuring equality." The hope was that we begin by redefining what is a "natural part of the human experience" and what is "normal" more broadly, and then shape our policies and practices accordingly.

The concept of equality, however, and thus achieving equity (the processes needed for assuring equality) remain fraught with complex challenges.

The key wording of Section 504 lays out a very logical corollary to the idea that individuals with disabilities belong among us, are us, and therefore need what all of us need:

> No otherwise qualified individual with a disability in the United States … shall, solely by reason of her or his disability, be excluded from the participation in, be denied the benefits of, or be subjected to discrimination under any program or activity receiving Federal financial assistance … (https://sites.ed.gov/idea/about-idea/#ADA)

Meeting the demands of those terms remains daunting to interpreters, even today, nearly fifty years after the passing of Section 504 in 1975. What did the legislators mean by "no otherwise qualified person" or "solely by reason of disability?"*

Elaine In the Legal Context

What makes Elaine "disabled," yet "otherwise qualified" to participate in the same educational programs as other students or to hold a particular job as an adult? Throughout Elaine's psychological and learning disability

---

* It is important to distinguish between specific "disability" among "otherwise qualified" students and a general "intellectual disability," or what we used to label as "mentally retarded" (a term no longer used in the DSMV and now commonly considered a slur). A comprehensive intellectual deficit that prevents someone from participating fully in an academic program does not constitute a "learning disability," for instance. The law does indeed recognize and provide, as yet imperfectly, for a fair treatment of such people, but their plight is substantially different than that of people who can perform at normal levels, if provided specific, appropriate accommodations.

evaluations (performed by qualified, professional diagnosticians, as per disability law), test scores have revealed two seemingly contrary things. One set of scores determines her status as "disabled." The other set determines her status as "otherwise qualified."*

The primary means of determining a "learning disability" (the sum effects of aphasia in Elaine's case) involves discovering a sharp discrepancy between a verified overall ability, as measured by a battery of sub-tests, and a marked deficit in a single or very limited number of sub-scores. In other words, the test taker proves that she or he functions within or above the average/normal range for other students in a public school system, for instance, but experiences a specific impairment that, without accommodation, prevents an average/normal level of achievement.

Educational records and testimony from the student and the parents also contribute to an ongoing diagnosis, but with essentially the same goal in mind: determining that the student is, indeed, qualified to participate, despite the disability. In other words, the student with a specific impairment may engage with their social, educational, or professional environment in somewhat different manner, but their interactions are nonetheless effective and normal.

Yes, She Can

Throughout Elaine's educational experience, Don and Barb worked hard to provide abundant evidence from a variety of professionals—doctors, therapists, teachers, and tutors—as well as personal testimony

---

* It is important to distinguish between specific "disability" among "otherwise qualified" students and a general "intellectual disability," or what we used to label as "mentally retarded" (a term no longer used in the DSMV and now commonly considered a slur). *A comprehensive intellectual deficit that prevents someone from participating fully in an academic program does not constitute a "learning disability," for instance. The law does indeed recognize and provide, as yet imperfectly, for a fair treatment of such people, but their plight is substantially different than that of people who can perform at normal levels, if provided specific, appropriate accommodations.*

from friends and acquaintances who knew or worked with Elaine. Such extensive personal evidence, when supported by professional evaluations, should carry great weight.

In one evaluation from 1996, the diagnostician made this note: "Elaine's thirty-four-point discrepancy between verbal and performance scores...render her Full-Scale IQ score to be meaningless." Furthermore, Elaine's "visual perceptual organization skills...are solidly average," while her "capacity for verbal concept formation was deficient." The testing administrator then suggested that Elaine would need "as much visual and concrete hands-on examples as possible," along with added processing time, but all with the assumption that she could then succeed in school from one grade to the next.

That evaluation confirmed, in fact, what Don and Barb had understood for a long time: Elaine was smart and also broadly capable enough to enroll in a public, general education program as a normal student while nonetheless needing help—accommodations or adjustments—that specifically addressed her challenges with language.

Again in 1998, at age ten as a fourth grader, Elaine underwent an evaluation of her intellectual capabilities. Her pediatric psychologist, Dr. Levesque, noted that Elaine had been tutored successfully at the Sylvan Learning Center at a fifth grade reading level and a fourth to sixth grade level in math skills. Her visual-motor skills tested above average, while her writing speed proved inadequate in the context of a typical classroom teacher's speed of delivery. Other doctors and educators reached the same conclusions regarding Elaine's intellectual abilities (as we will see later in the story).

Elaine was enrolled in early childhood programs from age two to five, all of which provided visual stimuli and individual attention, and all of which proved successful. Elaine again and again proved capable of mastering the same material at generally the same year-to-year pace as her fellow students. Her success depended, you might say, on three things: her innate ability, as proven by testing and in-school performance (her status as "qualified" under disability law); an extraordinary level of hard work on her part; and teaching methods that specifically addressed the effects of her aphasia.

A therapist in Arizona, Beth Jansen, working with Elaine when she was three years old, provided an early confirmation of that essential understanding of Elaine's capacity: "Elaine responds well to visual cues and seems to do best when manual sign language and gestures are used along with verbal cues...." With great consistency, Elaine performed well across the curriculum—and performs well now—when the teaching methods minimize or slow the flow of spoken words and maximize visual and tactile reinforcement of lesson material.

The aim of accommodation is not to lower expectations or in any way give a student an advantage. The aim, in theory, is to create a "level playing field," to provide adjustments to teaching methods and assignments or programs that make up for any *preexisting disadvantage* posed by a disability to an otherwise qualified and capable student.

The conflicts that embroiled Don and Barb with schoolteachers and administrators, especially during Elaine's third and fourth grade years, involved pedagogy—how best to teach Elaine, given her particular challenges with processing and producing language ("receptive" and "expressive" skills). What methods worked and did not work, and would teachers step outside of their accustomed teaching methods in order to accommodate Elaine and give her a fair and equal chance at success?

Teachers and school administrators responded variously, some with acceptance and creativity, others with frustration and resistance.

CHAPTER 6

Comfort, Complexity, Vulnerability

How the Yaqui Got It Right

Long before Elaine could form clear, conscious memories, her educational experience began with some adversity. While Elaine was a toddler, Barb had learned to anticipate Elaine's needs, despite Elaine's inability to verbalize them for herself. Some of Elaine's earliest preschool teachers noted Barb's ability to anticipate, and they expressed concern. If Barb did not press Elaine to express herself verbally but rewarded her non-verbal expressions, they reasoned, then Elaine would not adequately advance her verbal language skills.

Barb was unable to convince them that, in fact, Elaine communicated her needs very well, but in non-verbal ways, and that such communication need not interfere with verbal language learning. To the contrary, Barb insisted that Elaine's non-verbal communication helped advance her comprehension and thinking skills, thus providing some solid groundwork for building her verbal skills. There was no necessary either-or, as developing one successful mode of communication need not exclude or preempt learning another.

Barb's insight into the nature of aphasia resulting from prenatal brain injury may be relevant here: Elaine had experienced strokes that caused her aphasia *at or before birth*; thus, she was not struggling fundamentally with language recall, as someone whose aphasia comes later in life, but with initial language formation. Elaine was still learning language from scratch, so to speak—from visual and tactile experience while in the context of neurological damage. Thus, Barb could recognize and affirm Elaine's developing non-verbal expressions and build on those toward verbal expression.

In 1990, when Elaine was two years old, Don and Barb moved her to the San Ignacio Yaqui preschool in Richey Elementary (the Yaqui are a tribe indigenous to Arizona) within the Tucson Unified School District. While there, Elaine experienced a learning environment that, according to Barb's observations, she found more comfortable and entirely non-threatening. In the Yaqui school, teachers and children alike spoke their native language, as well as English and Spanish; but especially helpful for Elaine, the teachers heavily emphasized visual and tactile learning.

Also helpful, the school did not label Elaine as "a child with disability"; rather, teachers accepted her and each of the other students unequivocally, working with her merely as one more *normal* student with her own unique learning profile. During class sessions, teachers did not single out individual students and expose them to performance pressure. The children were free to help each other come up with answers and solutions. In that environment, "Elaine seemed 'zoned in,'" as Barb puts it now.

That sense of collective responsibility and communal identity obtained not only during school but also afterward. School programming included the home experience as well, with teachers visiting students in their homes and working with parents as a way of helping them enhance their children's at-school learning experiences. Families of students held parties for each other in their own homes, deepening Don's, Barb's, and Elaine's sense of acceptance within the learning community.

Another experience likewise strengthened Barb's sense of secure inclusion. Feeling perhaps overly concerned at first, Barb followed the school bus every day, wanting to ensure Elaine's safety upon arrival. She waited until she could see Elaine exit the bus and watched as teachers or staffers met her and led her and the other students safely into the school building. Barb would then drive back home, reassured. School personnel noticed Barb's presence each morning and responded by asking her to join the Parent Preschool Advisory Committee.

The teachers and administrators appreciated Barb's dedication and concern and came to value highly the practical suggestions Barb made about how best to teach Elaine. Among that group of parents and educators, Barb felt that she and Elaine were genuinely accepted and respected and felt "fully grafted in."

Elaine's IEP for that year carried a few simple yet well-directed learning goals. Elaine would participate in class activities, interact more comfortably with peers, and improve her motor skills. These goals served as means of reducing the tactile sensory defensiveness that hindered Elaine's progress in virtually every context.

As one therapist wrote in January of 1992, "It is pretty clear that Elaine is very much in charge of the foods she will eat." Certain textures irritated her, as did changes in her meal routine. "She refuses smooth food like yogurt, pudding, custard, and pumpkin pie...Cheese must be individually wrapped." Elaine ate fairly well, nonetheless, enjoying a limited variety of fruits and vegetables. She suffered no lack of appetite. "She is most comfortable," said the therapist, "when she can stuff her mouth full in mid-mouth and her cheeks."

One of her teachers, Mrs. Pinzon-Pitts, reported that Elaine was in fact doing very well toward those goals. She "participates during class circle time, asking questions during show and tell, responding to questions and singing the songs. Elaine enjoys playing outside and using the playground equipment."

Not everything at the Yaqui preschool functioned well. Neither Don and Barb nor Elaine recall any conflicts with teachers or tensions relating directly to Elaine. Their frustrations, instead, involved a more general issue. Several times, Barb asked the school administration if they could purchase more visual aids. Indeed, the school heavily emphasized visual learning. The process was fairly simple: accompanying text and terms with illustrative pictures, drawings, charts and graphs, timelines, etc., then helping a student make the connections. Elaine flourished. Each time Barb made the request, however, the administration declined, offering only vague explanations as to why they would not apply for the additional federal funds needed for such materials. Barb's uncertain recollection is that the administrators had made such applications to the federal government in the past but had consistently been denied the funds.

Nonetheless, the Schultzes recall their experience in the Yaqui school as overwhelmingly positive. In a letter to her brother, Barb recounts how Elaine had, at three years and three months old, learned to say "adoption." Jan O'Reilly, a pediatric physical therapist, and Beth Jansen, a speech-language pathologist, both noted Elaine's progress. "Elaine has demonstrated significant gains in all areas of development…Her attention span, play skills, speech, motor skills, tactile system, and motor planning abilities have significantly improved," wrote O'Reilly. Jansen reported that Elaine had "shown great progress over the last six-to-nine months in her use of expressive language."

O'Reilly and Jansen both recommended continued therapies for Elaine, emphasizing "sensory-based instruction." We recall here that assessment from Beth Jansen, the speech therapist in Arizona. Elaine showed "fluctuating ability to interact, process, and respond verbally. Elaine responds well, however, to visual cues and seems to do best when manual sign language and gestures are used along with verbal cues." For Don and Barb, Elaine's progress in learning and her comfortable interactions in the preschool were indicative of what teachers can accomplish with an aphasic student, given the right understanding, attitudes, cultural orientation, and tools.

New Lessons in the TUSD

Following her year at the Yaqui preschool, in the early summer of 1991, Elaine enrolled in the Tucson Project ABLE preschool program at Richey Elementary. There, a major shift in curriculum followed a shift from state to federal funding, delivering a sharp and troubling contrast between how the Yaqui worked with Elaine and how Richey Elementary school personnel would now deal with her.

The program change meant a new focus on developing verbal skills, at the cost of a diminished attention to visual and tactile learning. Thus, conflicts surrounding Elaine's innate abilities, challenges, and consequent needs reemerged between those who believed in Elaine while recognizing the complex challenges involved in educating her, and those who dismissed her as incapable of learning. In a context where Don and Barb hoped for thoughtful, knowledgeable assistance, they discovered new complexities and vulnerabilities for Elaine.

One of their first adverse encounters at the Richey Elementary preschool involved an impatient and irritable school psychologist. During the initial evaluation of Elaine, the psychologist became frustrated at Elaine's difficulty with following his verbal instructions. Growing exasperated and then giving up, the psychologist blurted out to Barb, "Elaine will never learn anything." The evaluation ended abruptly, by mutual agreement, but without a formal indication of Elaine's status as a child with addressable disabilities in a public school setting among her non-disabled peers.

That school psychologist had failed to consider a key factor despite urgings from Don and Barb. He failed to note the specific effects of Elaine's aphasia—that is, the language deficits that made following *verbal* instructions extraordinarily difficult for her. In other words, he apparently made the common mistake of equating a lack of verbal communication skills with overall poor cognitive function. More fundamentally, the psychologist failed to observe a basic principle of social science and of human interaction: "*Take time to know me*," as Elaine puts it.

In a report of June 6, 1991, a second school psychologist indicates a "Failed Child Find screening" as the reason for referral and reevaluation. The most likely explanation is that the second psychologist was issuing a subtle rebuke of the first for failing to do his job under the law. The IDEA Child Find provision requires every school to locate and evaluate, in a timely manner, those children within their jurisdiction who are suspected of having disabilities.

The Child Find process is triggered as soon as school personnel have reason to believe that a child has some disability and may need special education services. On the one hand, the requirement falls to the school district, not to the parents, and Elaine was new to the school. On the other hand, Don and Barb had already provided the school with abundant documentation of Elaine's challenges and needs, as well as of her capabilities and successes. Indeed, the first psychologist, had he done his job, would have generated all the evidence that he needed for establishing a diagnosis for Elaine.

Elaine Proves Herself

Elaine would soon prove the first psychologist wrong, despite the lack of a clear IEP and some learning delays throughout the following year. The reevaluation by the second psychologist shows Elaine testing at the "twenty-five-month level" (ten months below her chronological age, or six and a half months below, when factoring for her premature birth). Nevertheless, Elaine earned a certificate that same month for "Exact Signed English for Children with Developmental Delays." For that certificate, she learned numerous essential words (for instance, "grandma," "grandpa," "mom," "dad," "more," "please," "play") and learned to make simple sentences. Before learning to sign, Elaine would sometimes sit in the middle of the floor and cry, having grown so frustrated with trying to communicate with one of her family members. Her, Barb, and Anna learning to sign brought great relief to all of them. She otherwise performed reasonably well in her preschool year.

Don and Barb had geared up and found multiple sources of therapy and instruction for Elaine, as they would do again later in other school districts. In a letter to her brother and sister-in-law, Barb noted that they had her asthma under control, and they were working closely with a pediatrician and private therapists for speech, speech comprehension, and behavioral therapies. Jan O'Reilly provided weekly "sensory integration" treatment as well. Likewise, Elaine worked with Beth Jansen, a speech-language pathologist who provided weekly individual therapy sessions at the Schultz home. Jansen's reports affirmed Elaine's ability to learn, but also explained the specific nature of her difficulty with language.

According to Jansen, Elaine imitated motor actions well, "but refuses or seems unable to imitate sounds and words" and could not answer "wh" questions. Her verbal skills varied from day to day and rose or fell even within a one-hour session. In fact, her verbal skills seemed quite strong at times, but were vulnerable to overstimulation. Expressive and fluent at first, Elaine would eventually "shutdown" after twenty-to-thirty minutes of verbalization, seeming to lose her ability to speak at all.

At such points in a session, Elaine avoided further eye contact and withdrew emotionally. During these shutdowns, Elaine displayed a shorter attention span, became more physically active, and used visual signs instead of verbal words. Given time and rest, however, Elaine would return comfortably to verbalization.

Overall, Elaine made "great progress," according to Beth Jansen. Her prescriptions for Elaine echo what Don and Barb, the Yaqui teachers, and subsequent therapists, most teachers, and tutors affirmed: "Elaine will probably learn best by using visual cues combined with verbal/auditory cues." Elaine had made progress in physical and sensory therapy, while suffering only a few slight setbacks in speech and behavior therapy."

The School Proves Troublesome

Oddly, Elaine's initial Richey Elementary IEP for the 1991-92 school year designated her classroom teacher as the sole "person responsible." The IEP did not, however, include clear, specific recommendations for any classroom accommodations. Instead, it outlined a vague set of learning goals, providing only minimal indications of what the school, or the teacher in particular, should do for Elaine, in order to help her reach the specific classroom-related goals. In a small box on the IEP form, one note read "PT, OT, speech & feeding therapy."

Another troubling point on Elaine's first IEP, in preparation for her move into the regular Richey Elementary preschool, raised an old issue. The Special Education Department evaluator addressed Elaine's use of non-verbal communication. "Visual cues, some ASL (American Sign Language), may be used as a last resort if behaviors regress." The evaluator acknowledged Elaine's progress in interaction with peers; nonetheless, she observed that "language does not appear to have become an important tool for Elaine...little language is produced spontaneously," and, therefore, she issued a strong recommendation against use of ASL with Elaine.

This recommendation contradicted assessments made by O'Reilly and Jansen, which affirmed the need for visual cues as complimentary to verbal instruction. The evaluator described Elaine's intermittent and problematic use of language this way:

> On her "good" days, Elaine can play appropriately with others, use three- to four-word sentences to describe her play and to talk about pictures in books, ... and is very social. During her "bad" periods, she seems unable to cooperate or engage in play with others, ... does not use verbal speech, and refuses to try to imitate speech and is generally unresponsive.

In response, Jansen flatly rejected the position taken by the school's special education evaluator, whose recommendation seemed to rest on unsubstantiated theory, rather than on observation of Elaine:

> Sign language is viewed as a facilitator for verbal language, and not as its replacement. I have never met a child who continued to use sign language once he/she was able to use verbal speech. Sign language provides additional components or cues ... and does not replace the use of speech, but allows the child to gradually give up the signs as she is able."

Elaine's performance in the classroom confirmed Jansen's position. "When she is having difficulty using verbal speech, Elaine responds well to manual sign language and sometimes uses sign language during her non-verbal periods. She seems to understand directions and explanations best when signs are used."

Jansen also affirmed Elaine's general comfort within a small group setting, where Elaine could receive positive reinforcement from other children.

In other words, the keener observers understood a number of vitally important things: First, Elaine's difficulties did not stem from speech impediment or a lack of speech instruction. Second, encouraging Elaine to demonstrate her understanding by whatever means, whether through sign language or verbalization, was of paramount importance. Third, the use of visual cues and sign language did not hinder but rather helped Elaine develop her speech skills.

Misunderstandings and tensions surrounding that issue lay at the heart of Elaine's difficulties and Don and Barb's frustrations with school officials. For all that, Elaine had done well among the Yaqui and performed well again in the Project ABLE preschool, where teachers consistently made use of visual and tactile methods of instruction. According to her IEPs from these preschool years, Elaine integrated well with her peers while playing, talking, singing, participating in show and tell, and working in groups on classroom activities.

CHAPTER 7

Ready, Reset

A New Home Among New Friends

In the summer of 1992, the Schultzes moved to Belleville, Illinois, where Don would complete his obligation to the Air Force. Elaine adapted well to life in Belleville, especially at home and in her neighborhood. In those environments, she thrived. She remembers being overly friendly at times and loving to visit her new neighbors.

> *I remember in Illinois it was a fun place to go out and roam around. I had a lot of energy. It was safe to go from neighbor to neighbor. I remember that. I was 'guilty' of visiting neighbors out of the blue and my parents having no clue I was doing that. I was like "Hi, I'm coming in!"*

She felt no shyness and no lack of confidence.

Elaine recalls a particular friend name Nick who accepted her fully. "*He accepted me pretty quick. We got along really quick. We lived right across the street from each other,*" says Elaine. Their play was physically active, far more so than verbal, as well as bold and *normal*. They collected bugs, climbed trees, and snuck out of their homes in the late evenings and early mornings to roam their yards in the dark. "*We would do everything together. In the day, we found roly-polies and the skeletons of cicadas. They left their skins on the trees. Nick and I would compete to see how many we* could find. At night, we would catch fireflies. That was my favorite thing to do."

Nick never judged her nor, to the best of Elaine's recollection, was ever troubled by his own awareness of Elaine's differences.

Granting that an educational setting may challenge and highlight a child's learning capacities in ways that a home and neighborhood may not, it is nonetheless worth noting that Elaine functioned very well outside of school. She displayed no aversion to and no difficulty with socializing.

Elaine recalls another friend, Lisa, who lived in a trailer house "far away" from her and Nick. Elaine and Lisa spent some time in each other's homes but knew each other primarily from school. Like Nick, Lisa readily accepted Elaine without judgement.

> *I would see her at school mostly. She didn't judge me, and she even protected me a lot. I didn't quite understand why she did so, at first, but I figured it out. Most kids treated me very well, though. I couldn't speak like normal kids then, but that did not seem to bother most of the other kids.*

Elaine does not recall having any persistent trouble among other children, at home or at school. Her time with the Yaqui, in the subsequent preschool programming at Richey, and in her years at Douglas Elementary generally gave her confidence among her peers.

Ambivalence at Douglas Elementary

On the whole, Elaine's experience in the Douglas preschool program was positive. She felt excited about attending, enjoyed the bus rides to school, and liked her teacher, Mrs. Herbstreit. Don and Barb appreciated the teacher also, as she consistently proved eager to collaborate and was sensitive to Elaine's needs.

Like most children, however, Elaine occasionally struggled to adjust emotionally to her new circumstances. She displayed some fear of separation that, to Don, Barb, and the school psychologist, seemed less a response to any specific events at school than an ongoing developmental issue. Every year, near the end of September and into October, Elaine refused to go upstairs by herself at home or sleep in the dark. Shadows of trees frightened her. During that period each year, Elaine grew acutely aware of when Don, Barb, or Anna felt ill or suffered a slight injury. She wanted a bandage for every slight scratch of her own.

Before school one morning in September, Elaine wanted to stay home but would not tell Barb why. Barb insisted that she go to school. That day, understanding Elaine's distress, Mrs. Herbstreit kept Elaine out of recess. The two walked together and talked about her fears. Soon Elaine relaxed, adjusted, and seemed happy through the rest of the day. In Mrs. Herbstreit, Elaine found a compassionate and understanding ally.

Ambiguous IEP, Contrary Reports

The individual education program (IEP) guiding Elaine, her parents, and her teachers into the new year of preschool presented an ambiguous portrayal of Elaine. She sometimes preferred to work and play alone, but also seemed comfortable among her peers most of the time. She loved to sing. The school psychologist also noted Elaine's speech and language impairment, her "tactile defensiveness" in response to various textures of food and clothing, and her difficulties with physical balance. The psychologist added a somewhat disheartening assertion to Elaine's IEP: "Regular Preschool and At-Risk Preschool will not meet developmental needs."

Don and Barb responded by requesting a special ed placement for Elaine and, for the time being, asked Mrs. Herbstreit for ideas on how to help Elaine with spontaneous speech.

Reports from professionals outside the school system proved more encouraging. That November, an independent physical therapist recorded that Elaine tested "within the normal range" and did not need PT services. The following January, the school requested that the Schultzes have Elaine tested for hearing and vision impairment after an attempted test by the school failed to yield clear results. Then in March, a private audiologist determined in March that Elaine's hearing was normal.

And Yet, It Was a Good Year

Elaine remembers enjoying time among her peers on field trips and at parties with her peers at Douglas Elementary. "She was very engaging in those situations," according to Barb. The Schultzes had planned for a family weekend trip to Eckert's Apple Orchard in September. Knowing, however, that Elaine loved to spend time among her friends from school, they postponed their trip so that Elaine could participate in a visit to the same orchard as a school-sponsored field trip. "We felt it best to postpone our apple-picking adventure until after the field trip, allowing Laney to feel the excitement of learning for the first time with the class and then giving her the opportunity to teach her family!"

It worked. Elaine loved the field trip and excitedly told her family all about it when she got home.

Likewise encouraging to Don and Barb, Elaine eagerly brought home her artwork, repeating at home the show-and-tell that she had happily and comfortably completed in class. Elaine finished her final preschool year feeling upbeat and confident.

CHAPTER 8

A Sharp Downturn

That Kindergarten Catastrophe

While the kindergarten teacher's use of a slur in reference to Elaine stands out as a singularly egregious abuse, the whole kindergarten year weighed heavily on Elaine and her parents.

The teacher displayed a pattern of growing easily and quickly frustrated over Elaine's difficulty with verbal communication and thus with following instructions. She lacked patience; she responded curtly and disparagingly. Her manner of addressing Elaine tended to single out Elaine, embarrass her in front of the class, and leave her believing that she was "not smart." In this context, that essential distinction between a student meeting the *same standards* as other students, while yet meeting those standards *in a different way* carries great relevance.

What Barb and Don established was that Elaine did follow instructions quite well (when she listened), but in a round-about way, unlike what the other students did. They realized that in her frustration, the teacher often failed to read Elaine's work through to the end, marking the pages hastily with that "sad face" and moving on to the next student.

Rebuilding at Home

When Barb realized what was happening in Elaine's kindergarten class, she sat Elaine down one evening and promised that together they would "make the sad faces go away." Every evening, they reviewed the lessons of the day and addressed past lessons that Elaine had not mastered. Barb thus began a systematic repair, so to speak. Barb drew a large "brick wall," as she describes it, each brick being a skill that Elaine had mastered, and each gap a skill she needed yet to master. Little by little, Elaine filled in the gaps, until she had completed the wall and thus caught up with her peers.

Barb very soon noticed substantial progress. Of great significance in Elaine's development over her years of education, from preschool through college, was that Don and Barb noticed Elaine's high responsiveness to visual stimulation. Indeed, they had seen this even in Elaine's infancy and toddler years. They noted, too, again and again, Elaine's responsiveness to focused individual attention and to specific challenges with plenty of positive reinforcement.

Throughout her first five years of life, Elaine had battled her own innate limitations, especially her deficiencies with spoken communication and all the consequent frustrations. Barb saw this, of course, and as part of her remedy, she made sure to keep Elaine encouraged by helping her develop her own inner voice that told a different story than she heard from others. *"I do not remember much from my time in Arizona or even from early in Illinois, except that my mom always reassured me that I was not stupid. She let me know I shouldn't believe what some people said about me. It was a constant reassurance."*

Barb also began reading stories to Elaine about famous people with disabilities. The examples these stories provided Elaine of other people like her, living confidently and displaying self-efficacy, proved invaluable.

One story has stayed with Elaine to this day. Either late in her kindergarten or early in her first grade year, Elaine listened to her mother read about Helen Keller.

> *I loved the story of Helen Keller. My mom read many stories to me of other people with disabilities, and the story of Helen Keller inspired me. I liked her fight. She had a lot of courage. I like those stories,*

maybe because I always identified more with other kids who had disabilities. I didn't feel different among them.

Elaine had already developed a significant awareness of her differences. Now she was learning, both from her mother and from her experiences at school, a sense of toughness and accomplishment and an understanding that she could and would endure and persevere.

Kindergarten Ends with a Sigh

Near the end of Elaine's year in kindergarten, in April of 1994, the Belleville school provided Don and Barb with a standard progress report. The report begins with this statement: "The entire responsibility for your child's development cannot be assumed by the school. The home and the school must work cooperatively for his best interest."

The Schultzes clearly understood that and, as they had before and would for many years, remained deeply engaged in the education of their daughter.

While the report included an overall positive review, it also betrayed a frustrating lack of attention to Elaine's particular needs. Elaine earned the "S" for "Satisfactory" in nearly every category, but lower scores in two: She was given an "I," indicating improvement, for her "enthusiastic and willing attitude" for working and playing well with others and for speaking clearly. The teacher assigned Elaine one "N," however, suggesting that Elaine needed to contribute more to classroom discussion. Once again, the emphasis on socialization seemed to eclipse the possibility of a teacher shedding any light on the obstacles that stood in Elaine's path.

Adding to such frustrations for Don, Barb, and Elaine, the teacher demonstrated in yet another way her failure to acknowledge and address Elaine's specific strengths or needs. In her final comments, the teacher said, "Laney has greatly improved since coming to my class. Keep working on letter sounds."

Barb entered her own handwritten comments into the final evaluation, which affirm Elaine's overall positive experience in kindergarten, but which also reflect the Schultzes' ongoing frustrations:

> We are very proud of Laney's progress. It is our hope and desire that Laney will continue to find education to be (can and should be) fun, nurturing, and most importantly, a building up of her self-esteem. We will work with her in a positive manner. We certainly have praised her strengths.

Barb's underlining of "positive" and "strengths" likely served as a pointed reminder for the teacher. Neither Elaine nor her parents had forgotten the trauma Elaine suffered that year upon hearing her teacher insult her in front of her classmates.

Barb recalls that the teacher did apologize a year or so later, after she had a child of her own. Meanwhile, Elaine did not quite finish kindergarten. School administrators and her teacher seemed eager simply to move her on. Barb and Don felt sufficiently confident in Elaine's abilities that they agreed to press Elaine into first grade, but with a sigh.

Hope and Ambivalence

As preparation for the transition to first grade, and upon leaving the Early Childhood Program in the Belleville Area Special Education District, Barb and Don requested a formal reevaluation of Elaine. This evaluation, done in late April of 1994, also prepared them and the school personnel for completion of the IEP that would guide them into Elaine's first grade year. The Schultzes hoped for a reset. They hoped now that the school would be ready.

The school psychologist performing the evaluation commented briefly on the Early Childhood Program, which no doubt had some valid boasting points. The student-teacher ratio was low. Elaine spent half of each day in the special education program and half with the regular kindergarten class. The program provided speech and language services for what was acknowledged to be a language-intensive program.

The evaluation results for Elaine did not surprise Don and Barb at all: Elaine was an attentive, cooperative student who learned best when presented with lessons involving visuals and manipulatives.* She needed little cuing from adults. She was good at self-help and showed improved socialization. She spoke with a quiet voice when uncertain, struggled with language use, and tended to "echo" or "associate" with her peers, rather than respond directly to specific questions.

The overall test scores indicated that Elaine performed academically at an average to below average yet age-appropriate level, confirming her strengths in visual comprehension and non-verbal problem-solving, especially in pattern recognition (words, numbers, shapes). The evaluation also confirmed Elaine's specific deficits in verbal comprehension and expression. Of particular concern was Elaine's difficulty in following complex sequential instructions. Nonetheless, Elaine did significantly better, regardless of test type, given more time to process her thoughts and freedom from distraction.

The psychologist's recommendations followed those observations: Elaine should have individual help with language skills. Teachers should provide visual cues and demonstrations. Elaine should be as free as possible from distractions while testing and be given additional time for processing information. Assuming such accommodations would be in place, the psychologist believed that Elaine would be "successful within a regular educational setting."

Very near the end of Elaine's kindergarten year, Don and Barb met with school personnel for completion of Elaine's IEP. Once again, the Schultzes' collaboration with the school left them feeling ambivalent. While the education program included a substantial list of learning goals for Elaine, the plan of action for the first grade teacher and counselors was

---

* *I again avoid categorizing Elaine as a "visual learner" here, as we are addressing an aphasia-born verbal deficit, rather than a peculiar strength.*

general and vague: "special education and related services" and "speech and language therapy." The IEP did not include any other strategies specific to the disparity between Elaine's verbal and visual comprehension and made no mention of recommendations by Don and Barb, school psychologists, or doctors. The school's obligation to develop a more visual and tactile pedagogy remained unfulfilled.

Again, and as would happen throughout Elaine's public school years, school administrators and teachers failed to grasp an essential point of disability accommodation: It was they who needed to adjust fundamentally, not the student alone or the student most. Every anticipated step forward met with a stop.

First Grade in Belleville

Teaching methods would not be the only point of contention between the Schultzes and school personnel. During her year and a half in the Belleville school, she and her parents confronted a new question, one regarding appropriate classroom placement for Elaine. The IEP generated at the end of her kindergarten year provided this guidance:

> The student must be educated in the school where she would attend if not disabled, unless the individualized education program (IEP) requires other placement. Consideration must be given to any potentially harmful effect on the child or on the quality of services he/she needs.

Consequently, the IEP required that Elaine be placed in the general education classroom for one half of each day and in the special education classroom for the other half. In fact, the IDEA stipulates that a school should provide the least restrictive options possible, and thus students with disabilities should remain in general education (rather than special ed) as much as possible.

Ironies of Inclusion

Separating Elaine from her general ed classroom peers soon contributed to frustrations for her and for her parents. Indeed, she looks back at her status as a "special education" child as somewhat disabling. On the one hand, her movement in and out of the general ed classroom meant her identification with a group of stigmatized "others." On the other hand, inappropriate goals attached to her inclusion within the general ed classroom also led to stigmatizing.

Efforts toward equitable integration sometimes morph into subtle demands for assimilation. For example, many teachers value eye contact as indicative of a student's attention and engagement. For an autistic student or a student with anxiety disorder, however, eye contact might remain challenging and uncomfortable, if not impossible. That student might be paying close attention and learning on pace, nonetheless. Elaine often finds eye contact difficult to initiate and sustain, but she focuses very well, participates readily, and learns. Service providers in the disability services community often remind teachers that a common learning goal does not necessitate a uniform learning method or mode.

Barb believes the school's handling of Elaine exacerbated a complex of familiar problems, stemming from two things: an emphasis on "social passing" and on socialization, and inattention to Elaine's specific needs related to her disability. School officials facilitated "social passing," or moving kids forward regardless of preparedness or grades, so that students would not feel left behind. In so doing, the school failed complexly to meet Elaine's most fundamental needs as a student, indeed, as just one more student among her peers.

That emphasis on "social passing" manifested programmatically. For example, the Math Land program garnered displeasure from many parents. Children did not have to generate correct answers; instead, they merely displayed answers they could explain to the teacher in any way they chose. While school officials may have seen this approach as accommodating, parents had no way of knowing if their children were in fact learning. In Elaine's case, this meant a lack of concerted effort to ensure that Elaine learned what she needed to learn, compounding the challenges she already faced. The emphasis on social passing, rather than on mastery of the material, in other words, meant a lack of careful attention to Elaine's struggles as a student with aphasia.

Furthermore, the emphasis on "social passing" echoed an older, familiar misconception among Elaine's past teachers and counselors. In Belleville, school personnel insisted that Elaine merely needed greater socialization. Don and Barb found this misemphasis frustrating because it was contradictory, given another accommodation mandated in the IEP. Efforts toward socialization were somewhat thwarted by the dual classroom placement. While Elaine felt comfortable among the other children in the general ed classroom, she was the only student in her grade that year receiving special education services (and only one of about half a dozen such students in the entire school). Thus, her placement in the special ed class left her feeling stigmatized and limited her time with students in the general ed classroom where broader socialization might happen.

Elaine does not remember her time in the Bellville school system warmly. "*I hated school in Illinois. No one could understand me.*" At home, she felt safe and understood. She had her parents, her sister, and her friend Nick.

Had the Belleville school administrators, teachers, and counselors acknowledged Elaine's difficulties with language comprehension and expression as indicative of a thoroughly diagnosed disability, they might have avoided many of their own frustrations. The issues of placement and pedagogy would arise again soon in Montana, where they would become the central points of dissension between the Schultzes and the Montana City School district.

CHAPTER 9

New School, Old Troubles

First Grade in Montana City

After the year and a half in Illinois, midway through Elaine's first grade year, the Schultzes moved to Montana City, Montana. Elaine began her tenure at the Montana City elementary school pleasantly in January of 1995. Her teachers had prepared the other students for her arrival, and the students proved "extremely accepting of her," noted Barb, despite her language delays and shyness.

Elaine recalls one exception among the students, a girl named Brianna.

She was my only first-grade bully. She knocked me down in recess, but all the kids ganged up on her. She never did that again. I think she was going through a rough phase. I don't know what it was. I'm pretty positive it had to do with family. We got along after we got older.

A counterpoint to Brianna, Kendra somehow grasped the nature of Elaine's challenge and taught Elaine to tie her shoes. Kendra's patience and method of teaching impressed Elaine. "*She SHOWED me how,*" says Elaine. "*She seemed to understand that I was a visual learner, and she showed me how to do a lot of things.*"

For the most part, Elaine felt comfortable among her new classmates, and it seemed that kids at Montana City school were generally more accepting and respectful than kids had been in her Belleville classes. In both locations, however, it was the adults she encountered who made her life difficult. Professionals bring their expertise, hard earned and well applied, to their students. They also bring their common failings as human beings. Sometimes the net result is that a professional may see a student too narrowly through the lens of a particular discipline and sometimes compound that error when, despite the expertise, respond to a new challenge with dismissiveness.

Seeing, but Not Seeing

As she had done in Arizona and Illinois, Elaine worked through an evaluation with a psychologist, this time for the Montana City School through the associated Prickly Pear Special Services. The psychologist clearly recognized the profound discrepancy between Elaine's low verbal skill scores on the one hand and her overall intelligence on the other. Elaine scored especially well on visual and tactile learning tests. According to the evaluation, Elaine performed well and comfortably with written and hands-on questions, but she lacked confidence during the verbal-skills testing. She grew tired quickly. Unwilling to persist through that phase of testing, Elaine would simply say, "*That question is too hard.*"

Noting Elaine's difficulty with receptive and expressive language skills, the psychologist recommended speech/language services, "with emphasis" on verbal language skills and "strategies for supplementing auditory memory skills." Frustratingly, he made no clear or specific mention in his report of Elaine's need for visual and tactile learning.

Likewise, he failed even to acknowledge Barb's recommendation that those working with Elaine should pursue some education about students who displayed learning challenges specific to Elaine. He noted that Elaine "shuts down" when presented with too many letters and words, yet he said nothing in response to a note from Barb indicating that Elaine "really wanted to try reading if she liked the pictures." The psychologist saw Elaine, yet he did not see her well. That is to say, while his observations gathered the full range of relevant details about Elaine's condition, those observations did not yield a coherent understanding of Elaine's condition, let alone a diagnosis or an adequate academic plan.

A Teacher to Remember

Apart from that disappointing evaluation by the psychologist, things began well for Elaine at Montana City School (MCS), mid-way through her first grade year. Her new teachers communicated readily with Barb and did seem to understand Elaine's need for an adjusted pedagogy that emphasized the use of visuals and manipulatives. They worked hard to instruct Elaine accordingly, and Elaine made significant progress in her phonetic skills, decoding, and spelling. Among Elaine's school records, homework, and pictures from first grade in Montana City, two things still catch Barb's attention: a "Student of the Week" certificate and a little book that Elaine assembled about Helen Keller. Even now, Elaine recalls her first grade teachers with affection.

Elaine's first teacher at MCS stayed with the class for only a few weeks, but even that brief presence gave Elaine, Don, and Barb a sense of hope. She was attentive, thoughtful, and interested in addressing Elaine's unique challenges. She left an impression. *"I remember her face. She had curly blond hair and was tall and thin. She was nice."* She was pregnant, however, and Elaine learned that her pregnancy involved complications that forced her to leave. Katie Jenson, a twenty-something substitute, stepped in. She too proved memorable for Elaine.

We may forget—or believe we forget—most of what we learned in school. Indeed, we typically make that complaint with an eyeroll. More likely, we fail to understand the benefits of those past learning processes, of learning to think, observe, catalogue, and evaluate our knowledge, and then to speak and write it effectively. That, despite whatever specific subject details we do truly forget.

Certainly, on the other hand, we remember essential characteristics of those teachers who shape us. Elaine remembers Katie Jenson as *"another mother figure making sure I was okay."*

> *I have a lot of fond memories. Haha, I remember sleeping in class once. I didn't mean to. I was supposed to listen and practice cursive writing, but I dozed off without knowing it. I think most kids would have been woken up, but she just let me sleep a while and then finally said, "Okay, time to wake up." I was like, "How long have I been sleeping?" I was embarrassed. I remember her always being a gentle lady.*

Elaine and Katie still connect. *"When I get to see her every once in a while, we remember each other as if it were yesterday."*

Katie eventually had three children, including her first daughter, Ali, who also had some disabilities. Katie's awareness of the difficulties Elaine faced in the public school setting helped prepare Katie for her own daughter's journey through the school system.

> *I think she remembered what my mom said and all the situations I went through over the years. She was aware of how I was treated by other adults sometimes. She didn't want her children to go through the same things. She understood my barriers to communication, while most people just thought I was lazy. It was more that I didn't know what was going on, so I really couldn't participate as much as I wanted.*

Elaine attributes her positive recollections of her first grade semester in Montana mostly to the classroom work of her teacher, Katie Jenson.

Elaine remembers, nonetheless, her exhausting struggle to learn, to match the classroom pace, and to meet the demands of homework. For teachers and parents alike, seeing past the "good grades" proves difficult, even with school children who carry no extraordinary challenges. Elaine could not express herself adequately, so she felt reluctant to tell anyone how difficult school truly was for her. We may not think of the "rigors" of kindergarten or first grade, but we easily miss the emotional and mental intensity that learning even the most basic things can mean for a student with profound learning differences or disabilities. With each year that passes, schoolwork becomes more difficult, of course, and by design.

For Elaine, the challenge of keeping up grew emotionally unbearable. Elaine "held it all in," as Barb notes. Elaine knew she was not keeping up; she was not fitting in. In fact, she was not fitting into the school curriculum, the teacher's expectations, the system.

Second Grade and Stress at Home

In late August of 1995, enrollment in second grade brought additional challenges to the Schultz family. During Elaine's first grade year, Barb had begun experiencing depression and anxiety, which intensified the following year. She struggled to redefine herself after Don finished his graduate work, completed his term in the Air Force in Illinois, and began his career as a pathologist in Montana.

For a time, settling into their new home and new school district had kept Barb focused and busy with a strong sense of purpose. With all of that behind her, however, she felt directionless and unsure of herself. While Elaine seemed to be doing well enough at Montana City School, Barb recalls that she and Don were not as involved in Elaine's education as they had been. The demands of transition and adjustment to a new town, a new school, and new jobs had exhausted them. They felt reassured, on the other hand, by Elaine's productive spring semester in first grade. Consequently, neither of them were seeing Elaine so clearly as they had before.

Elaine's emotional health began to slip. She continued to work hard on her school assignments, but under an increasing weight of depression and anxiety. She did not know how to express her deepening fears and frustrations; thus, Don and Barb could not help her process those emotions.

After several weeks of Elaine's first semester in second grade, however, Barb began noting signs of inordinate stress. Elaine frequently complained of headaches and tiredness. She dreaded going to school. She worked hard but showed none of her typical enthusiasm for learning. Barb realized that, in fact, Elaine's anxieties and exhaustion were intersecting her own. Elaine needed help; Barb needed help; so, she found a therapist for them both.

The therapy sessions proved revealing. As Elaine learned from the therapist how to articulate her anxieties clearly, both to the therapist and to her parents, Don and Barb grew increasingly alarmed, indeed, frightened that they might lose Elaine. They learned from Elaine that she was experiencing panic attacks and frequent suicidal ideation. Elaine remembers telling her parents, "*I don't fit in. I'm not right. Life is too hard.*" The ongoing therapy sessions proved vitally important for Elaine and Barb. At home, Don and Barb refocused, determined again to pay very close attention to Elaine's emotional health.

The signs of stress that Elaine displayed began to multiply. "*I was really a mess,*" she recalls. She suffered daily severe headaches, a throbbing pain in her temples that grew more intense as she struggled harder to understand her teachers and keep pace with the other students. "*When I had those headaches, I just couldn't think. It's like I couldn't hear well or see well either.*" The same headaches occurred following any stressful periods or incidents that involved strong emotions. Embarrassed at falling behind or frustrated with another student who could not understand her speech, Elaine felt inescapably different and deficient. She began grinding her teeth, biting her nails obsessively, and chewing gum constantly for relief.

Ambivalence

Despite her emotional distress, she did not feel mistreated by her classmates or her teacher, Mrs. Chambers. Thus, her second grade classroom experience prompted an ambivalent emotional response. She says of that year, "*The other kids and the teacher were nice enough, so in that regard, second grade was mostly positive.*"

Elaine's manner of responding to her inner distress was to lash out. "*Second grade was also my phase of being rebellious.*" Elaine remembers developing "*a hot temper.*" Two things lay at the root of her anger as her second grade year began. For one, she felt confusion about no longer seeing Katie Jenson in class. "*I was angry about that, and I did not want to follow the rules anymore.*" Katie had been patient and gentle in the first grade class, and she had made thoughtful, creative responses to Elaine's atypical learning processes.

Despite Katie's compassion and competence in first grade, Elaine had also come to feel hopelessly different. "*I just wanted to be normal,*" she recalls. Elaine knew that she could not talk normally like the other kids could, and she developed a habit that troubled her.

"*I would repeat a word or sentence when I didn't mean to. I didn't have a stutter. It was a weird repetition. I know kids were aware, but most of the kids were gentle with me.*"

Elaine's Montana classmates, both in first and second grade, did not tease her much; less, in fact, than her Illinois classmates had. "*They seemed to understand that I was just a scared little girl who didn't talk.*"

Perhaps we should remember a common fallacy here when tempted to make "a distinction without a difference" in regard to students with disabilities. Yes, Elaine's classmates saw a distinct difference in Elaine, but they seemed nonetheless to accept her fully as one of them. She belonged.

Despite kindness from most of her classmates and from Mrs. Chambers, routine communication became an unbearable ordeal.

> *I got so frustrated that other people could not understand me and that it took me so long to understand them. I would say, or sometimes yell, 'Stop talking so fast. I can't keep up!' I wanted to just 'get it' now and understand what was going on. My temper would flare.*

Elaine's high level of self-awareness fueled her frustration. "*I was aware of how behind I was,"* she recalls, but she could not adequately express or explain her dilemma.

Her disability dogged Elaine relentlessly, no matter which way she turned. She began wearing glasses in second grade, but each eye required a different prescription. *"Visually, I'd lose track of words in a paragraph."* Indeed, she struggled with reading. She knew that she read too slowly, which frustrated her, and remembers thinking often, *"Why should I bother? I'm trying, but my head hurts."* Elaine noted, too, that her textbooks had become more complicated. *"Oh my gosh! That's so many words,"* she would say to her mom.

Likewise, when her teacher wrote on the chalkboard, Elaine could not see the words well unless she sat close to the board. In response to questions from her teacher, she often said, simply, *"I don't know."*

"I played possum a lot," she recalls. *"I'd just stay quiet and not let on that I didn't understand. I didn't want to explain that I couldn't see the board."* Once again, she did not want to bring embarrassing attention to her differences and difficulties.

Ironically, Elaine's description of her reading difficulties reveals both her fundamental ability and the impact of her particular disability: *"I couldn't understand what I read or even wrote. I would memorize the pattern of words and even the motion of my pencil, but still not understand the words. I had to see an object to match a word with. Then I would understand and remember."*

Elaine needed her teachers and school counselors to see those unique learning patterns more clearly. Some did; some did not.

Elaine's classmates and her classroom teacher responded gently and with patience, but not all of the adults did so. Her gym teachers accused her of being lazy, and to Elaine they seemed persistently *"loud and scary"* as well as insensitive and impatient.

> *We had two gym teachers, a man and a woman. I never got along with the woman. They would take turns, and neither one could remember my name. I remember one time when I got in trouble for*

trying to help my friend Erica. I had a weird habit of trying to help people. I was trying to get a stink bug out of her hair. She hated bugs and started freaking out, so I was carefully pulling it out of her hair. It took a while, and the PE teacher got mad that we were not paying attention.

Elaine had to sit on the side, prohibited from any further participation in gym class that day. She felt confused about what she had done wrong. "*Erica was trying to explain about the bug and defending me, but the gym teacher didn't listen.*"

Gym class offered some occasional relief, despite the teachers. Elaine looks back with a smile at a few things. "*I liked the physical movement. I could throw and catch balls and run, but I couldn't jump rope!*" Nonetheless, she usually dreaded gym class, in part because of the teachers, but also because too many of the activities excluded her full participation. More to the point, Elaine's gym teachers gave rapid verbal instructions that confused Elaine, and they made no effort to find alternative ways for her to participate. If she struggled with an exercise, the gym teachers expressed frustration, humiliated her verbally, and made her sit it out.

Finding Her Strength

Despite her emotional stresses and cognitive difficulties, Elaine was not, in fact, shy or afraid. "*I was pretty short,*" she says, "*but that didn't stop me.*" She could be bold when she felt compelled to be so.

I was a little overprotective of other kids sometimes. I hated bullies because I knew what it felt like to get bullied and pushed around. I saw someone trying to force a smaller boy off the swing. I had a sort of flip-switch temper, and I would get angry. I told the bully to stop, and I think I scared him with my anger and all of my confused verbiage. I was about to knock him down.

Fortunately for the bully, and perhaps for Elaine as well, Mrs. Chambers intervened.

Elaine found a reliable source of understanding, comfort, and guidance in Mrs. Chambers. "*She was another teacher who was like another mother,*" says Elaine. On one occasion, Mrs. Chambers had to step in and quell a conflict that erupted in class.

> *I had a big misunderstanding with Erica. I had invited her and other students to my birthday party, but apparently Erica did not get her invitation. I told her that I wanted her to come, but she was hurt and accused me of lying. That really hurt me. I wanted her to understand that I just didn't communicate well, so I just walked away from her in class. She was crying.*

Other girls joined in, chastising Elaine for being "horrible" to her friend. Her quick temper ignited, and she blew up. "*Why are you guys ganging up on me?*" she yelled. Mrs. Chambers pulled Erica and Elaine aside. First, she helped Elaine explain herself to Erica, but then compelled Elaine to apologize in front of the whole class and sent her to the principal's office.

Erica and Elaine did not speak to each other for a week. "*That was my first fight with anyone at school. I got so mad. I just couldn't say anything clearly. Erica misheard me. I probably sounded like a dork.*"

Throughout the ordeal, Elaine did not feel like she was in trouble with her teacher. Instead, Mrs. Chambers' patient, gentle, and calm manner freed Elaine to do what she needed to do. "*I needed to learn how to forgive people who couldn't understand me. That was a really big lesson for me then. My temper really was about the communication barrier, and I wasn't very forgiving. I knew I was different; I just didn't want to be, so I got mad.*"

In reflecting back on that experience, Elaine knows that her temper covered a deep sense of embarrassment. It took her a while to let go of her anger at Erica, but eventually, the two girls reconciled, and Erica attended Elaine's party. They healed the rupture in their friendship. Elaine was tough, but now she had learned to be tough in a new way.

Like Katie Jenson in first grade, Mrs. Chambers proved to be among Elaine's best teachers in terms both of grasping Elaine's peculiar challenges and of creatively accommodating Elaine in the classroom.

> *I had a good experience because she reminded me of my mom. She was like, "take this, you are going to do this." She let me know when I was misbehaving. She wasn't rude, just a mother figure. Stern, serious, "You are going to do this today. You are going to do this now."...I wasn't nervous with her. I just was, like, "Okay, I better not fight with you because you sound like my mom. I can't get away with anything."*

Elaine knew that Mrs. Chambers believed in her, and she pressed Elaine to accomplish what she could. "*She just wouldn't give up on me.*" Mrs. Chambers understood the underlying causes of Elaine's anxiety, dealing firmly but gently with her on those issues as well. "*Mrs. Chambers gave me a lot of confidence.*"

Critically important to Elaine's growth through this year was Mrs. Chambers' understanding that Elaine did not need pity or leniency because of her disability. Like every other student, Elaine needed to face behavioral standards common to all students at the school, and thus she needed occasional discipline. Whether from pity, fear of litigation, or fear of displeasing a student or parents, a teacher might make excuses for the disruptive behavior of students with disabilities. Elaine benefited from a teacher who did not suffer such fears. Elaine knew it then, and she is quick to recall it now.

A review of Elaine's classwork and homework from that year reveals a productive learning experience, despite Elaine's intense inner struggles. Mrs. Chambers annotated Elaine's classroom and homework papers with encouraging responses, both personal and academic. She also made a variety of adjustments for Elaine, especially in taking the time to give Elaine the essential, individual attention that she sometimes needed.

> *I remember that she occasionally gave me extra time. She was patient with me. Sometimes she would come back and help me understand*

the assignment. If I didn't understand the grammar in a sentence, she would help again. At that age, I didn't really understand why, but I was learning that repetition was a big deal for me.

With encouragement from the teacher, Elaine's classmates helped her as well.

Elaine understood very clearly at that age how she learned more easily through visual presentation than through verbal and textual instruction. Mrs. Chambers also recognized Elaine's unique learning profile, and with her guidance, Elaine came to love drawing and painting. She excelled artistically. Elaine's classroom and homework papers are replete with pictorial illustrations of the text, some produced by her teacher and some by Barb, but many by Elaine herself.

A Hard Point Driven Home

In November of 1995, Elaine began regular sessions at the Sylvan Learning Center. Her experience there reinforced her progress in the Montana City School, and evaluations by her Sylvan teachers also confirmed her learning strengths and challenges. According to Christine Chapman, Sylvan Learning director and instructor, Elaine showed increasing confidence, love for exploring new things, joy in picture games, and noteworthy skill in reading short passages. Chapman noted also that Elaine displayed no apparent attention deficit.

On the other hand, Chapman confirmed that Elaine grew uncomfortable in large groups of people, disliked verbal games, and struggled with reading long passages. Elaine was a perfectionist, and any failure to understand quickly and keep up left Elaine frustrated. She often withdrew into silence after saying, "*I don't hear you,*" her way of saying, "I don't understand." She dreaded any classroom circumstance that might highlight her difficulties and lead once again to her feeling different, as if she did not fit in.

One experience drove home for Barb the cognitive and emotional limitations that Elaine faced. Wanting to cooperate with the school's emphasis on socialization, Barb decided to explore what Elaine might learn from more exposure to other people. She took Elaine to a ball game early in her second grade year. At the game, Elaine did not seem ill at ease with the mere presence of other people, even in such large numbers. At first, while fans came and went and sat making conversation, Elaine responded confidently, and she interacted happily with those around her. Barb felt encouraged.

Very quickly things went awry.

Shortly after the ball game started, the intensifying noise became problematic and then traumatic. People were cheering, of course, but also yelling angrily. Elaine grew distraught, believing that people were expressing anger toward her. The great confusion of language and the emotional intensity clearly frightened and disoriented her. She could not process the high-energy, fast-paced experience adequately. Barb and Elaine had to abandon the ballgame. Elaine had not attended such a noisy and raucous event before, but her responses to noises in the crowd echoed her responses to the noises of a classroom.

And Yet the Misfocus

Despite Elaine's friendships, the good rapport and shared success between Katie Jenson and Elaine in first grade and similar successes with Mrs. Chambers throughout second grade, other school personnel had begun focusing on Elaine's supposed need for socialization.

Elaine often remained quiet, diffident, and occasionally withdrawn, so administrators, counselors, and psychologists insisted that more socialization was, after all, what she needed most. Time, personnel, and other resources they allocated on Elaine's behalf served mostly to reinforce that emphasis, rather than reinforcing her need for a well-resourced visual and tactile pedagogy. Once again, a failure to focus on an individual student's noteworthy and well-documented differences would lead inevitably to inadequate responses among key professionals.

The final IEP from second grade, dated March 20, 1996, presented a mostly positive report on Elaine. She had some difficulty in distinguishing details from main ideas in her readings and did not always comprehend her readings well. She also had some trouble with math on the Woodcock-Johnson test, despite enjoying math and otherwise doing well in the subject. On the other hand, she read orally at grade level, displaying good decoding skills. She made good progress toward understanding and following written instructions. She had also made progress in sentence composition and identifying nouns in sentences.

As Elaine's second grade year came to an end, Mrs. Chambers completed a final academic report, affirming Elaine's progress.

> Elaine uses phonetic skill very well…We continue to encourage Laney to verbalize more…I am thrilled with Laney's spelling preparation. She does well on tests and works without adaptation in this area…We have used sentence webbing to help her organize ideas. This has worked well…She is drawing solutions to multiple-step math problems.

Mrs. Chambers praised Elaine highly for her hard work, her willingness to do more work, and her faithful smile. "I have loved my year with her," she wrote.

Elaine's academic record in her second grade year, satisfactory though it was, did not reveal the level of effort Elaine expended nor the intense emotional stress she experienced. While Elaine's first grade and second grade teachers had done well, they had not fully appreciated the causes or depth of Elaine's struggles. Elaine continued to spiral downward emotionally. Unfortunately, the next year school would only deepen the crisis.

CHAPTER 10

A Deepening Crisis

Third Grade

Elaine began her third grade year with a deep apprehension that Don and Barb shared. She had experienced some academic success in second grade, but her memory of almost constant frustration welled up as she again confronted a new teacher in a new classroom. The coming year would confirm Don and Barb's fears, presenting additional and intensified challenges. Fortunately, a few of Elaine's educators became close allies.

Elaine had begun working with Sandi McGuire, a licensed clinical professional counselor and education specialist with a private practice, at about the same time she began third grade. Sandi's counseling center provided a vibrant and varied learning environment, especially well-suited for Elaine. She and the other kids could play freely with dolls and polaroid cameras. They could push their hands through wet and dry sandboxes, molding and refashioning shapes. Sandi had carefully constructed her center for effective, individualized teaching and close observation. Elaine thrived in the highly tactile and visual setting.

An Unrelenting No

Despite Elaine's progress at Sylvan, Sandi recognized very soon that Elaine "was clearly going down and down" emotionally from conditions at the public school. She tried many times to consult with administrators and teachers, including the special education teacher, but without success. "Montana City School teachers and administrators refused to listen," she recalls. Rhonda Filmore, school principal and Jessica Willett, district superintendent, both insisted that the school offered an adequate provision of FAPE (free appropriate public education) under the Rehabilitation Act and the IDEA. Moreover, they insisted that they would not accept recommendations from experts outside of the school and had no legal obligation to do so.

Don, Barb, and Sandi all agreed on a key observation: MCS personnel believed that they understood better than anyone else what Elaine needed. They refused to hear Don, Barb, Sandi, or any of the professionals who would eventually speak out on Elaine's behalf.

On the other hand, Sandi noted that MCS had geared up impressively for dealing with an anticipated influx of autistic students. This followed a national trend among schools at the time from elementary through college levels. Nonetheless, MCS administrators remained unresponsive to Elaine. This struck Sandi and the Schultzes as ironic, given the fact that Elaine was just one of only five or six special education students enrolled at the school and the only one in her own grade. Why would the school invest in students not yet there, but refuse to invest substantively in a student already with them?

Sandi describes the rigidness of MCS officials. "They would not deviate from what they did for all students. I would plead with them to try this or try that. 'No, that is not how we do it here' was their response every time."

Over and over, MCS administrators refused to adapt to Elaine's special needs, hardening their stance, perhaps unwilling to engage in personnel training and pedagogy revision on behalf of just one student with an unusual disability.

Even now, Sandi McGuire recalls, with a noticeable exasperation in her voice, the relentless "no" delivered by the school administrators:

No, Elaine could not use a keyboard; every assignment had to be handwritten.

No, the school would not produce additional visuals for in-class instruction. "That is not how we teach here," they answered.

No, the school did not need outside help. They openly expressed resentment toward Barb for providing visuals of her own.

No, the school would not provide a listening device or other assistive technology, fearing that Elaine would become dependent on it.

No, the school could not allow shortened days.

No, the school could not accept instruction at Sylvan as a substitute for instruction at MCS.

Unlike their counterparts in Illinois, the MCS administration denied an alternative placement provision for Elaine. While Elaine's experience with a special education placement in Belleville was problematic for her, Don and Barb believed that Elaine needed some relief from the daily pace and distractions she encountered in the MCS classroom. She was again shutting down frequently, especially as the weekdays progressed.

Elaine carried a heavy schedule. In addition to her regular classes, she spent four hours each week with a tutor, three hours at Sylvan Learning Center for math and reading, plus two hours of scheduled study each weekday evening with her parents.

Hoping to ease Elaine's schedule without sacrificing any of the essential help, Don and Barb asked for a limited adjustment to Elaine's regular attendance schedule: Monday, Tuesday, Thursday, and Friday with the other students in the classroom, but Wednesdays with Sandi McGuire and with teachers at Sylvan. The Schultzes, Sylvan, and Sandi all provided documentation that the instruction delivered to Elaine on Wednesdays would be at least the equivalent of what she received in the public school.

The principal and superintendent refused to compromise, insisting that such substitutions violated state and school regulations regarding school attendance.

An Untenable Daily Reality

Meanwhile, Don and Barb exhausted themselves through their efforts to keep Elaine on pace with her classmates. They had noticed in the fall that Elaine was not comprehending much of her classroom teacher's verbal material. In April, Barb wrote a letter to the school administration, explaining again the problems they were seeing: "We are constantly hearing from our child, 'It's too hard.' 'I don't understand.' 'I'm stupid.' At night with the help of a tutor, Don and I reteach all the subjects visually."

Within a few months, the relentless pressure, effort, and frustration took a toll on Don and Barb, but especially on Elaine.

In the context of under-resourced teachers and programs, along with an administration resisting more robust accommodations, one can expect teachers to feel highly stressed, even overwhelmed by new, unfamiliar challenges. Elaine's third grade classroom teacher, Mrs. Smith, responded with ambivalence. On the one hand, she reported liking Elaine as a "sweet" student and observed that her classmates liked her as well. Early in the year, however, she stated explicitly to Barb and Sandi McGuire that she had never wanted to teach above the kindergarten level and did not want to work with disabled students at all. What hope that Don and Barb felt for a positive public school experience began to sink.

Despite her troubling confessions, Mrs. Smith made some genuine efforts on Elaine's behalf. In her reports, she noted both strengths and weaknesses. In the plus column, Elaine displayed an impressive skill on the computer. Indeed, Elaine recalls her work in the computer lab as a highlight of her third grade. "*I didn't care about recess. I got obsessed with playing math and computer games.*" Once she learned a math concept, she retained her understanding well. She could learn and remember single words well also, and she typically stayed on task during class. She had no apparent attentional difficulties unless confronted with too much verbal information.

Through her daily observations, Mrs. Smith grasped at least the general shape of Elaine's cognitive challenges. She understood that most of Elaine's struggles involved language comprehension and expression. On the other hand, Smith failed to grasp fully the nature of Elaine's disabilities and consequent needs, and she seemed unable to address those needs effectively. Smith wondered if Elaine merely suffered from a hearing impairment, and she registered a persistent frustration with Elaine. "It takes so many different ways to get her to understand a new concept," she complained. She felt convinced that Elaine did not understand the concept of prime numbers, for example, despite noting that Elaine somehow grasped the underlying pattern within the numbers. Elaine had an extraordinary ability to see patterns, in words, numbers, and pictures. Mrs. Smith had missed a vital clue.

According to Sandi and Barb, Mrs. Smith remained rigid in her teaching methods. Her accustomed pedagogy may have been valid for most students, but it was not a good fit for Elaine. Barb sent a letter to Mrs. Smith, pleading with her and her colleagues to pursue a deeper understanding of the obstacles Elaine faced and of how she learned best as a student with aphasia. Their collective resistance, which manifested in IEP meetings rendered fruitless by redundancy, poor listening, and weak follow-through, had long since grown exasperating. Of course, Don and Barb knew that a full solution ultimately lay with the administration's embrace of the challenge posed by Elaine. Her teachers needed additional training and resources.

Nonetheless, Barb appealed to Mrs. Smith to do what she could and suggested a few changes in method. In her April letter to the administration, Barb also noted problems with Elaine's homework assignments. She recalled a typical occurrence. "Elaine brought home her science book with what appeared to be written definitions of science terms. When we asked Elaine to tell us what she needed to do, she said, 'I don't remember...I'm stupid.'"

Barb further pleaded with Mrs. Smith to send clear instructions home with Elaine, preferably enhanced with simple hand-drawn pictures, so that Elaine would know how to complete her homework assignments.

In her self-reporting, Mrs. Smith expressed several concerns, betraying a lack of that clearer insight that Don and Barb had hoped from her. According to Mrs. Smith, Elaine rarely initiated contact with her classmates, did not seem to socialize comfortably, and usually played alone. As the fall semester progressed, Elaine preferred to stay indoors and work in the computer lab, rather than play outside with the other children at recess. Mrs. Smith observed that Elaine participated willingly in classroom activities, but only if she understood what was going on.

During recess and in the classroom alike, Elaine's responses to visual cues were quick and on point. It troubled Mrs. Smith, however, that Elaine relied too heavily on watching the other students, as she looked for cues from them about what to do. Mrs. Smith seemed to understand that Elaine's struggles involved language comprehension and expression, yet her routine instruction remained overwhelmingly verbal. "Elaine gets confused when the teacher speaks in long sentences," as Dr. McCormick would record later on.

Frustratingly, Mrs. Smith did not use a textbook for math. She made limited use of pictures and manipulatives, but she relied heavily on her own verbal delivery. When she believed that Elaine could not hear her well enough, she would stand beside Elaine, touching the relevant page of homework. She reported that this helped Elaine "stay on task." Barb felt that "Mrs. Smith's understanding of visual instruction was weak. Laney was not learning sufficiently. 'On task' does not equal learning!" Elaine quickly fell behind on her homework. "*I was so far behind in reading, math, just about everything,*" she recalls. "*I just couldn't keep up.*"

Elaine had already come to understand that she learned far more easily if she could use her hands and match words to pictures and objects. Once again, however, a teacher could see Elaine but not see her clearly. It apparently did not occur to Mrs. Smith that Elaine's withdrawal socially might indicate deepening emotional stresses or a greater ease of learning alone on the computers. Mrs. Smith's observations seemed tantalizingly close to a recognition of Elaine's state of mind, yet frustratingly off point.

Elaine Begins to Crumble

In her first several weeks in third grade, Elaine fled her new class and sought refuge in the second grade room with Mrs. Chambers. "*I wanted* to go back to second grade," she says with a chuckle and a sigh, "*but of course they explained to me that I could not do that. They were nice; they obviously had no choice.*" Mrs. Chambers gently persuaded Elaine to say put while offering her some regular comfort. She made sure to catch Elaine in a hallway or during recesses and ask how she was doing, knowing that Elaine was not doing well.

Elaine's headaches, teeth-grinding, and nail-chewing worsened. She developed another problem, resulting somewhat from stress and somewhat from a prescription of steroids as treatment for her asthma. Elaine began to eat. "Eating was the only thing she could control for herself," says Barb, and she soon became steroid dependent. "She would puff up like a balloon sometimes" from the steroids. She ate voraciously. One teacher asked Barb, "Don't you ever feed her at home?" while they understood the effects of steroids, says Barb. "The teachers seemed unable or unwilling consider that Elaine's circumstances at school might be contributing to her stress."

The recurring issue of Elaine's failure to keep up with homework along with her difficulty in following complex verbal instructions led to increasing stress between Elaine and Mrs. Smith, as well as between the Schultzes and the school. Elaine and Mrs. Smith's relationship suffered, and she does not remember her teacher favorably: "*She had the outward appearance of being kind, when parents came to visit, but as soon as they were gone, she was a different person toward me. She was good with most students, but she focused mostly on the ones that were able to do the work easily.*"

It seemed to Elaine that Mrs. Smith paid only a begrudging attention to her. Elaine recalls that "*things were really going downhill then.*" Mrs. Smith seemed exasperated, as if "*she didn't know what to do with me anymore. She just wasn't listening.*"

As each day ended, and likewise each week and each semester, Elaine felt more burdensome. "*Mrs. Smith couldn't wait until I was out of there. We didn't exactly fight; we just never got along. She didn't know what to do with me.*" Elaine cannot recall Mrs. Smith ever speaking abusively to her or about her in front of the other kids, but "*when we were alone together,*" she says, "*that is when I knew.*" Her teacher's demeanor and tone of voice hardened. "How many times do I have to tell you this?" she would ask, or "Do I have to tell you this a fifth time to get you to understand this?"

Elaine talks about her third grade experiences now with a somewhat self-disparaging tone: "*I'm sure I had that dumb look on my face, like, what do you want me to do?*" That frustrated people. It frustrated Mrs. Smith especially. "*When it came to me, I was driving her bonkers with not keeping up. That began a phase when, if I didn't understand, I thought I didn't have to do the homework. That was a bad excuse, I know, and I was thinking it out loud. I guess I should have kept that to myself.*"

Elaine's instincts clashed with Smith's efforts at nearly every point. Mrs. Smith did not approve of Elaine staying indoors during recess, for instance. She worried that Elaine was not socializing enough, but Elaine knew that by working on the computers, she could learn.

> *I think I made her uncomfortable. I remember when I stopped going to recess. I didn't care any more about what we did in class. I just wanted to enjoy something at school. All of a sudden, I discovered computers with Math Blasters, Jumpstart, and game-like programs that taught grammar and writing skills. It was a fun way for me to learn. I could type in answers, see pictures, and hear the computer voice repeat the answers back to me over and over.*

On most days, Mrs. Smith could eventually persuade Elaine to leave the computers and go outside. "*She wasn't angry,*" says Elaine, "*but she would keep telling me that I had to join the other kids for recess. 'C'mon, let's go. You can't sit here all day,' she would say.*"

Whatever foibles may belong to Elaine's third grade self, she needed the professionals around her to step up and be flexible and creative. Ironically, the same educators who were gearing up for an influx of autistic students could not, would not see or hear Elaine. In the meantime, Elaine was learning to facilitate her own learning; she found in the computer labs, not a refuge from other kids at recess, but a refuge from the teacher and a place where she could achieve mastery.

A Precocious Insight

Elaine's keen self-awareness and clear understanding of her circumstances led to a moment of insight. One day after school, she asked her mom to spend a day in class with her, so that Barb could better understand the stresses that she felt. Barb realized the value of such a visit, so she came to school with Elaine and spent a day observing. It worked.

Barb already knew quite well what Elaine needed, but her visit to the third grade clarified her vision of the environment in which Elaine struggled to learn. Through much of the day, Elaine's classroom was a jumble of movement and voices. Teachers and students shifted frequently, both mentally and physically, from one activity to the next. They did so at a speed that suited the teacher's need to cover the required material. Barb understood that this at times frenetic pace reflected the pressure under which teachers worked, and she continued her efforts on that front. She felt compelled, nonetheless, to appeal to Mrs. Smith as well.

Late in the day, during a recess, Barb had seen enough. She confronted Mrs. Smith. Elaine was asked to leave the room, while Barb and Mrs. Smith had a talk. Elaine did not hear the conversation fully or clearly, but she noted the tension. *"I couldn't hear everything my mom was saying, but it was obvious that my mom was not happy with Mrs. Smith. I did hear her say something about not letting me fall through the cracks."*

Elaine could not possibly keep up under her current circumstances, explained Barb. Elaine had no fundamental comprehension issues; nor did she suffer any abnormal attention deficits. No, she was *not* hearing impaired. She simply could not match the pace of Mrs. Smith's heavily verbal instruction and could not adequately sort through the extraneous noise. Elaine's best efforts ended again and again and again in frustration.

Elaine's difficulty with speech left her even more vulnerable. *"I usually dreaded school,"* she says now. She could not articulate her frustration or her pain. She could not explain. She could not *say*. *"I didn't dread it so much in first or second grade, but in third and fourth, I did. I couldn't speak *properly. I had to stick with basic words to get people to understand me. I had to be repetitive with words. I talked funny back then."*

Elaine is thirty-one as of the writing of this book, but those memories from twenty-four years ago remain fresh. She still struggles sometimes.

I still don't talk like a normal person. Now, the more tired I get, the more I slur like I'm drunk. I know then it is time for me to go to bed. I can't read well. Sometimes I can't understand what people are telling me, and I misinterpret. That still happens today. Someone will say to me, "That is not what the teacher said—or friend said, or doctor said." When it happens, it reminds me of my childhood.

Elaine could not clearly articulate her frustrations or her needs; but, in any case, it seemed that few at Montana City School were listening to her, to her mom, or to anyone else.

CHAPTER 11

A Legal Fight Takes Shape

Long before Elaine began third grade, she had developed a keen awareness of her differences. She had grasped the essential reason for her struggles among her teachers and her fellow students. Although the tense conversation she overheard between Mrs. Smith and Barb gave her some insight into what her struggles meant for her parents, she did not know, on the other hand, the extent of the battles they were fighting on her behalf. During one interview with Elaine, I asked her if, in third or fourth grade, she was aware that her parents had retained an attorney. "*I wouldn't have known what that meant,*" she said.

> *I just know there was a lot of change, especially in fourth grade. Then I wasn't seeing a lot of my peers as much. I would see them in the morning and through lunch, but then be gone most of the day, working with a tutor. I remember being frustrated by that. All the bigger conflict was in the background for me.*

Don and Barb carefully protected Elaine from that larger conflict. At home, she was aware that her parents talked together about her school, but she overheard little and understood little of what she heard.

Questions of Evidence

Elaine's case revolves first around questions of evidence. Did the evidence that she and her parents presented establish that she had disability? If so, then how did that disability manifest itself? That is, in what ways did it limit her basic life functions (communication and learning, for instance)? Despite her disability, was she still "otherwise qualified" to participate fully in an educational program alongside other students?

Don and Barb had diligently amassed a substantial body of evidence over the years. With the help of doctors, counselors, teachers, tutors, and friends, they established that Elaine did indeed work with some disabilities. They and Elaine had just as clearly demonstrated that she belonged in school as a normal student. She could learn well in a public school classroom if administrators and teachers would acknowledge her abilities and appropriately address her disabilities. Don and Barb had the law on their side. They had the evidence. And yet, they still had to fight.

The IDEA, ADA, and Rehab Act have no proactive enforcement from any government agency or from any federally mandated executive body within a school system. No one outside of the IEP team checks the quality of the IEPs. If parents do not feel satisfied with either an IEP or with the follow through by school personnel, they can appeal for mediation with a state office of public education or with the federal Office of Civil Rights, or they can hire an attorney.

Powerful Testimony

Don and Barb felt boxed in. On the one hand, the Montana Office of Public Instruction (OPI) informed them that they could, at public expense, pursue a reevaluation through the school district. Furthermore, according to the OPI, the school district must consider the results of a reevaluation in any decisions the IEP committee would make regarding the implementation of FAPE requirements. On the other hand, Don and Barb did not feel especially trusting of MCS officials by that time. They recalled what the school principal had said about the IEP team not accepting outside expertise. Would another in-house evaluation benefit Elaine?

After repeated failed attempts to persuade administrators and teachers in the Montana City School, Don and Barb found another substantial source of help for Elaine. Despite the earlier warnings from Principal Filmore, Don and Barb decided to have Elaine reevaluated by a private, clinical psychologist at their own expense. They hoped for a clearer understanding of the underlying causes of Elaine's difficulties and for a substantiating body of professional documentation.

Don initially felt concerned about the financial cost of testing, but Barb had mustered some persuasive help from the Montana Advocacy group along with assistance from several educational and medical professionals she and Don had consulted. Don agreed that they would pay for the reevaluation. They needed some powerful reinforcement; then, perhaps, school officials would feel compelled to listen.

Dr. Annette McCormick delivered. Over a two-day period in January of 1997, she conducted a thorough examination with Elaine "in order to document Laney's learning style and to provide recommendations for educational, therapeutic, and medical management." Her evaluation also drew on interviews with Don and Barb, MCS teachers, Sylvan teachers and tutors, two speech therapists at the school, and Elaine's medical and educational records.

Dr. McCormick conceded that aphasia is not necessarily an obvious disability. It is, like many others, "invisible." MCS personnel failed, nonetheless, to take Elaine's case seriously, despite the carefully amassed evidence presented to them. They responded, instead, by insinuating at times that Elaine may be "retarded" and insisting that she merely needs more "socialization."

McCormick carefully built a psychological and educational profile of Elaine as a fundamentally normal and healthy child. Throughout the testing, she noted, Elaine felt safe and confident. McCormick's testing environment and methods provided Elaine with a dramatic relief from her feelings in and about school. "Laney does not present as significantly depressed, anxious, or in any way traumatized," although "she did convey a sense of her own 'differences.'"

Throughout the testing, Elaine performed extremely well one-on-one when given time to express herself and given positive, affirming feedback. She displayed no memory deficits, retaining what she successfully encoded. Her visual memory proved especially sharp. Her sense of direction was strong. She demonstrated solid non-verbal reasoning skills. She loved magic, math, and science.

When Elaine was six years old, Don and Barb took the girls to a magic show in Las Vegas starring Lance Burton. Both girls loved the show, but Anna, being far more adventurous than Elaine, went up on stage as a volunteer for a magic trick. She won a box of tricks but gave it to her sister. Elaine recalls being fascinated by the tricks she saw Burton perform and learned some of the tricks in the box that Anna had won. She also recalls discovering that the tricks were a lot harder to learn than she had anticipated.

McCormick also noted that Elaine seemed entirely free of attention deficits, impulsivity, and hyper-motor activity. She was highly organized. She had a strong sense of motivation. She could remain focused on a variety of activities for a long period of time, losing focus only when overwhelmed by excessive verbal stimulation. Elaine was not "lazy," displaying no aversion to hard work; indeed, she was a perfectionist. She tended to set "unrealistically high goals" for herself and became self-deprecating after any sort of "failure."

Elaine also expressed to McCormick her long-standing frustration over feeling "so misunderstood by many people working with her." Elaine knew, despite feeling "stupid" and despite the word "retarded" still echoing in her memory, that she could learn, if only…

Through her exhaustive evaluation, McCormick confirmed Elaine's status as a child with disabilities and provided a specific diagnosis: aphasia. After she completed the testing process, Dr. McCormick paused, looked Elaine in the eye and said, "Don't ever let anyone tell you that you are stupid. In your Indian tribe, you would be a princess."

Repeat, Repeat, Repeat

McCormick's assessment reconfirmed, with great specificity, much of what other professionals had previously concluded about Elaine. McCormick wrote, "Laney has been evaluated numerous times over the years, and there is consistent documentation of verbal skills falling significantly below non-verbal abilities."

At one year of age, Elaine "was found to have average intellectual abilities with mild motor, speech, and language delays." Again, at three years and eight months old, "Laney was noted to respond well to visual cues," but struggled with imitating sounds, and she regularly "shut down" after twenty-to-thirty minutes of verbalization. At age six, through testing with Prickly Pear Special Services, Elaine demonstrated the same noteworthy characteristics.

Now, midway through third grade, Elaine proved strong on visual measures but weak on verbal. In fact, McCormick's testing placed Elaine in the first percentile on verbal skills, but in the ninety-second percentile for visual comprehension and expression. Elaine could, in fact, retain and follow complex instructions if presented with appropriate cues.

Frustratingly for the Schultzes, one speech therapist working for the school disagreed, after a semester of meeting with Elaine in weekly twenty-minute sessions. She concluded that Elaine did not retain information well, regardless of how she presented material to Elaine. Instead, she believed that Elaine merely experienced a significant memory deficit. A review of the therapist's methods, however, revealed two problems. First, the therapist had not provided Elaine adequate time. Second, after presenting material to Elaine with a combination of verbal and visual methods, the therapist had not employed any visual prompts in testing Elaine's recall.

McCormick specifically called into question the MCS speech therapist's earlier assessment regarding Elaine's supposed inability to learn and retain information. "Asking Laney about a story she had read earlier with the help of visual clues is still a verbal task if the current request for recall is entirely verbal." About a year later, Dr. Levesque, the pediatric psychologist responding to a crisis in Elaine's development, would say much the same: "Elaine did much better [in test recall when] pictures were present to match the auditory information provided."

A different therapist, working for Sylvan Learning Center, conducted speech and language testing with Elaine. She noted that Elaine seemed shy at first but warmed up and grew confident once she understood the therapist's plan for her. On the one hand, Elaine struggled to understand basic questions, and she found open-ended questions especially difficult to answer. She did not perform well on word finds or recalling word sequences, and she displayed some paraphasia (a production of incorrect sounds, words, or phrases). As verbal testing continued, Elaine would eventually withdraw, saying, "*This is too hard.*"

Nonetheless, Elaine responded successfully to word tests when presented with corresponding images. During such testing, Elaine often said, "*This is a fun game. I like this.*" Thus, the Sylvan therapist confirmed a strong correlation between teaching and testing methods on the one hand and Elaine's performance on the other.

McCormick's more thorough assessment of Elaine confirmed and strengthened those conclusions. In response to verbal tests, Elaine tended to say, "*This one is too hard.*" While she easily recalled overall shapes, she showed some difficulty recalling internal details. According to McCormick, this is an ironic but common trait among students with verbal processing challenges. Predictably, Elaine showed great difficulty with repetition of sentences immediately after hearing them, yet she learned as well from verbal as from visual prompts, if given adequate time to process and repeat the information correctly presented to her. She did well on "sound-symbol" tests, for which she could associate a sound with an image.

Elaine did well identifying details in pictures, sequencing images, and "copying complicated designs by memory," according to McCormick. Furthermore, "Her error awareness was excellent. Thus, her visual perceptual abilities were well developed. Laney could immediately see what a puzzle was supposed to be when she looked at the individual pieces, suggesting good 'right hemisphere/Gestalt' abilities. Laney's visual memory skills are highly developed."

McCormick confirmed what Don and Barb had known since Elaine's earliest toddler years: she demonstrates normal intelligence and ability *visually*. In the context of that understanding, McCormick concisely articulates an essential insight into the typical classroom instruction: "It is important to realize that almost any activity is language activity."

Visual, Visual, Visual, Please!

Based upon that insight, McCormick laid out a set of recommendations for Don and Barb and for Elaine's educators. "Concepts need to be taught visually along with words so that Laney can encode the information." Teachers should use words sparingly, being careful to deliver short, clear, and concise instructions. Manipulatives and images used as prompts for recall are essential. Teachers and therapists should be very careful to avoid verbally overstimulating Elaine, as she will "shut down." McCormick conceded that a shutdown might at times be an avoidance tactic, but she likened it to "blowing a fuse" in an electrical circuit. For Elaine this served as a coping mechanism. It was a matter of emotional survival.

McCormick did agree that Elaine should learn to initiate interactions with her classmates more confidently. The greater focus should remain on appropriate pacing and correct pedagogy, however. Here McCormick seemed to take aim a second time at the school's own speech therapist: The therapist should take thirty minutes each week to consult with teachers and other therapists, as a team approach should be integral to working with children experiencing "complicated neuro-developmental issues." Elaine needed patient instruction as well, from teachers with a clear understanding of her abilities and disabilities.

McCormick praised Don and Barb highly for their insightful work with Elaine, but she offered a caution to them as well: "It will be helpful for the parents to tolerate a certain amount of struggle on Laney's part to see how she can come through a situation. Interventions should be kept to a minimum...This is hard for parents of aphasic children, as there is a tendency to overprotect."

Her advice for school personnel was a bit more direct: "Laney needs 'a full language evaluation by a speech pathologist who specializes in aphasia.'" McCormick noted, too, that such testing should precede the development of suitable learning strategies for Elaine.

Allies

Don and Barb immediately followed through on Dr. McCormick's advice, and an independent speech pathologist began meeting with Elaine, during her third grade year. The pathologist worked closely with Don and Barb, helping them to create effective teaching materials, focusing especially on images, patterns, words, and sequencing of ideas. She expressed one concern in particular that echoed McCormick's thinking: Too many teachers and tutors with too many diverse strategies may be overloading Elaine. Elaine's educators needed to work as a team with a coherent plan and a consistent approach.

As we noted before, the fragmented nature of Elaine's school days became exhausting and agonizing. Her movement in and out of class, working among the other students, stepping out to work with a resource teacher, then working with outside help after school hours exhausted and confused her. The hectic schedule often cost Elaine her recess times as well, so she did not get the emotional and mental relief the other students enjoyed. Don and Barb had appealed to the school for an adjustment to her schedule but without success.

Fortunately, Elaine had allies, both within and outside the Montana City school. Together with Don and Barb, they would all help build the case for Elaine. Besides Mrs. Chambers, these allies included staff at the Sylvan Learning Center, a variety of psychologists, doctors, counselors, and tutors, and also Terri Ortlund, Elaine's early third grade resource teacher.

Terri understood, empathized, and spoke boldly on Elaine's behalf. She once told Barb that the failure on the part of teachers and administrators to address Elaine's difficulties amounted to abuse.

Elaine felt fragmented, divided between her schoolwork under the stressful tutelage of Mrs. Smith and her time spent learning joyfully through the inspiring care of Terri Ortlund.

I felt pretty lazy in third grade unless I was with Mrs. Ortlund. With her, it was a different story. I made an effort. If I was in class, though, I didn't care. I didn't care about homework or reading a book. The only thing I cared about—obsessed about!—was my spelling. I was a perfectionist, so that is what I would study the most because that is where I struggled the most. In class, I didn't put much effort into math, science, or any topic.

Terri took time to learn how Elaine functioned, how she learned, and how she communicated. She knew to be patient and to experiment. She knew also to keep encouraging Elaine and building up her self-confidence.

Terri Ortlund insisted that Elaine was "a very capable kiddo" who was making good progress. She also insisted that her colleagues should pursue a better understanding of Elaine's disability and engage in more education in how to help Elaine. The parents, school personnel, and other professionals involved needed to provide Elaine with a stable placement and coordinated help.

Elaine discovered other allies in her fight. She had begun attending Sylvan in the summer before third grade. There her teachers understood her. They specialized in innovative and individualized education. She remembers liking the environment and liking George, her first tutor.

Mom was not able to teach me more math and science, so she took me to Sylvan. I took a test to begin with. They were surprised at how advanced I was in math after working with my mom. They discovered that I had learned some college level material. The tutors were great at one-on-one tutoring, and George was good for math and English.

Another tutor, Elisa Gaither, proved especially helpful to Elaine. Like others at Sylvan, Elisa understood Elaine's challenges and responded deliberately and effectively. In fact, Elaine does not remember anything negative from her experiences at Sylvan.

The program directors at Sylvan wrote a letter to Don and Barb in June of 1997, praising Elaine for her "steady progress." She successfully reviewed third grade supplemental math skills, mastered skill gaps in word analysis, and had already begun working on fourth grade reading comprehension skills. Elaine demonstrated, as always, "a strong desire to learn" within a nurturing environment, and she was steadily becoming "more extroverted and expressive" and "more confident in her oral reading skills." The Sylvan directors also confirmed what the Schultzes and other professionals had long noted: Elaine is a visual learner.

One Sylvan instructor, Rena Foley, provided Don and Barb with some powerful testimony. She, too, confirmed Elaine's learning style, and she laid out a strategy for MCS teachers that cut to the heart of the matter. She urged MCS administrators to allow Elaine more time out of class for individual instruction, free of the distractions that typically trouble aphasic students. "Such problems do not occur at Sylvan," Foley noted. She also pointed out that Elaine socializes well both at Sylvan and elsewhere, offering a pointed rebuke to the ongoing and misinformed emphasis on "socialization."

Rena Foley cited Elaine's "tremendous progress" and suggested a systematic approach to instructing Elaine. Limit instructional sessions to fifty minutes, each followed by a five- to ten-minute break. Back off when Elaine grows frustrated and try a variety of methods when she struggles. Provide thoughtful guidance but never grow impatient and never give

Elaine answers. Respect her sense of self-efficacy and her need to develop independence. Indeed, Elaine tends to work well on her own until she needs help. Remember always to provide pictorial clues to accompany words; drawing pictures to associate with vocabulary words is essential.

In September of 1997, Dr. John Levesque, pediatrician, evaluated Elaine and contributed his report to the mounting evidence. He explained the causes and effects of aphasia specific to Elaine. He recommended that Elaine should attend regular class but for a shorter time each day. He suggested that she attend only core classes or take a mid-week break so that she could attend speech therapy and instructional sessions at Sylvan without overloading her school days. She needed regular relief from the stress of classroom noise and pace. She needed time.

For Don and Barb, all of this proved frustratingly familiar and redundant, as one professional after another reaffirmed the results of past evaluations. Convincing MCS administrators and teachers remained a challenge. Levesque wrote his report as an implicit affirmation of Terri Ortlund's earlier assertion that Montana City School's poor responses to and neglect of Elaine constituted abuse. By this time, however, the resource teacher that Elaine loved, Terri Ortlund, had lost her job. In the early spring of 1997, MCS let her go.

Into the Long Fight

In June of 1997, another of Elaine's tutors wrote a letter to Rhonda Filmore on Elaine's behalf. Don and Barb Schultz were "aware of their daughter's limits," she wrote, and she then provided an eloquent testimonial of Don and Barb's collaborative spirit, humility, sensibleness, and respectfulness toward educators. She also praised the Schultzes for the hard work they had done for Elaine. In other words, Don and Barb were not the problem.

That letter from a tutor followed, by one month, a letter that Don had written to Principal Filmore. Don began his letter forcefully: "We are exasperated and feel that the agreements set forth in our daughter's IEP are not being held to as stated and written…We sat at the February meeting and felt that finally we were being heard, and now we see that this is not the case."

Barb recalls that, by the middle of third grade, the frequent IEP meetings had grown exhausting and exasperating. They led to no clear plan, no definitive action, and no measurable, positive results for Elaine. This, despite the fact that the meetings involved teachers, counselors, and the school principal.

In his letter, Don carefully and systematically reminded Principal Filmore of the IEP terms and of the school's failure to comply. The school had agreed to maintain regular communication with the Schultzes about Elaine's progress, but in fact their communication was sporadic and fragmented. The school had agreed to a two-week notification before quizzes and tests, but those notifications did not come. The school had agreed upon alternative testing formats, involving visual prompts, but such testing formats were not usually given.

In one meeting, the school agreed to change the word "should" to "will," in reference to agreed-upon teaching strategies. Nonetheless, the pedagogies did not change. Tests were generally not given visually, and Elaine would come home with essay questions for completion of her science tests. Don responded: "We request that Elaine not take a science test until it is in accord with the agreements stated in the IEP. If you have any questions, please do not hesitate to contact us."

Don explained the contrasts between Elaine's experience in the MCS classroom on the one hand and her experience with Terri Ortlund and with a sympathetic speech pathologist on the other. From Terri and the speech pathologist, Don and Barb could count on regular, clear progress reports. Elaine also brought home well-conceived and effective visual instructions with her homework. In contrast to that, Don explained, "We are not always able to [communicate well] with Mrs. Smith." On the matter of visual instruction, Don's comments grew very specific: "We are coming to realize that Mrs. Smith does not understand what it means to teach visually. One does not stand over a science or social studies book and point to a picture while speaking and call this visual teaching."

Don praised Mrs. Smith for trying hard and treating Elaine well in class. He acknowledged that she allowed Elaine to sit close to her and often gave Elaine some illustrated learning materials that were already available in the classroom. He noted that Mrs. Smith even paid a visit to the School for the Deaf and Blind, hoping to learn some helpful strategies. "We feel that she cares and is a good educator, but we strongly perceive that she needs assistance in teaching and testing our daughter appropriately," Don wrote candidly, struggling to maintain an even tone.

Late in the summer of 1997, as Elaine began the fourth grade, Rena Foley, one of the Sylvan Learning Center teachers, provided Don and Barb with a deeply encouraging assessment of Elaine's progress at MCS through the end of third grade. Rena's perspective summed up much of Elaine's development, in fact. "I have seen Elaine progress from a timid, introverted child who needed constant one-on-one attention into a bright, outgoing fourth grader that resents extra help because, as she says, 'I can do it on my own.'"

Sandi Ashely remembers that Elaine did indeed contribute significantly to her own progress, especially after learning how to articulate her distress. "You learned to communicate with me and your parents very well about the troubles you were having. You were a key part of the process, El."

CHAPTER 12

Expectations, Claims, Realities

Throughout Elaine's third grade year and all the way to the middle of fourth grade, the Schultzes and their allies did battle with the school. An attorney, several personal friends, a new resource teacher, and more medical specialists joined their effort. Meanwhile, Elaine maintained her difficult academic progress while suffering her emotional decline. Altogether, Elaine, her parents, and her teachers would eventually reach a definitive crisis point.

In her January 1997 evaluation of Elaine, McCormick acknowledged the "difficult balance between keeping Laney included as much as possible in mainstream education and pulling her out." She urged Montana City School officials, therefore, to craft an agenda for subsequent IEP meetings. They should, she suggested, outline three priorities: communication, socialization, and academic assistance. Specifically, useful strategies should follow each priority along with clear expectations for parents, teachers, therapists, and administrators.

Letters, IEPs, and More Letters

In April of 1997, Don and Barb sent a letter to Principal Filmore and Superintendent Willett. Recalling advice from the Montana Office of Public Instruction, they wrote, "After much deliberation, we contacted a lawyer and had our daughter privately tested by a neuro/clinical psychologist." They then expressed the crux of their frustrations.

> In December, we called an IEP meeting. We must tell you, honestly, we felt placated by everyone attending that meeting, with the exception of Mrs. Ortlund, Christine Chapman (director of Sylvan), Alexis Flynn (private speech pathologist), and Marina Lemieux (private tutor). What an awakening to realize that the educators our child came into contact with on a daily basis had written her off. In their minds, she had reached her potential.

They had much more to say in their letter, addressing the numerous specific issues underlying their frustration.

Don and Barb addressed the firing of Terri Ortlund, Elaine's beloved special education teacher. They praised Terri as "an awesome resource teacher" and appealed for her rehiring. They briefly reviewed Elaine's challenges and described the transformative nature of Terri's work. Following McCormick's diagnosis of Elaine's disability as aphasia, Ortlund had called another IEP meeting. Her own follow through on the recommended pedagogy had produced remarkable positive progress for Elaine according to the Schultzes. "The last grading period showed wonderful results," Don and Barb explained. Subsequent to that second meeting, the instructional team produced "the first IEP [report] where all the goals were either mastered or at 85% or higher. This is a first in our daughter's academic career."

The Schultzes further noted how they had repeatedly demonstrated to the school that Elaine learned best and learned well visually. "We looked back through all her past individual education plans (IEPs), and repeatedly it was noted that our child learned best visually." They explained again how "Mrs. Ortlund listened to us and worked with us," ensuring that under her instruction at least, Elaine benefited from appropriate teaching methods.

Furthermore, Terri had taken her professional responsibility very seriously. "We are thankful for Mrs. Ortlund," the Schultzes wrote. "She learned as much as possible about childhood aphasia. She connected us to the School for the Deaf and Blind and spent a day there with us, learning how to help Elaine." Terri also spent time with Don, Barb, and Sylvan instructors, creating effective visuals for Elaine's lessons.

Don and Barb related how Terri's work had taught Elaine great confidence, joy, and ease with her classmates, both in class and on the playground. "For the first time, [Elaine] feels understood in what we can easily imagine was and is still at times an extremely lonely world." Again, in that letter to Willett and Filmore, Barb urged the school to rehire Mrs. Ortlund for the coming school year, Elaine's fourth grade.

Prior to handing her copy of that letter to me, along with other documentation for this book, Barb added a handwritten note about Terri Ortlund: "They let her go. She gave us all the files, and she was the one who had told us to get an attorney."

The Legal Battle Opens a New Front

Another letter soon reached the school principal, Rhonda Filmore—this time from an attorney, Lynn Hanley. In his letter of June 9, Hanley laid out his plan. He would assess all past services provided by the school for Elaine. He would review all past IEPs. He would help the Schultzes and MCS together "in determining the appropriate level of relevant educational services for their child and ensuring that these services are delivered in a timely and collaborative manner." He then requested access to all school records pertaining to Elaine and all records that in any way referred to Don and Barb Schultz. He would also attend the IEP meeting scheduled for June 11, 1997, subsequently delayed until June 25.

In his preparation for that upcoming IEP meeting, Hanley wrote a second letter to Don, Barb, and school officials. He addressed several concerns that needed their attention. First, the turnover among the school's resource teachers threatened continuity of instruction. Elaine had three different resource teachers in two and a half years. Likewise, turnover meant the loss of familiarity with Elaine that a resource teacher gains over time. Hanley also questioned administrative support for teachers, noting the lack of collaboration among teachers and administrators and the antagonistic posture of school officials, who rejected "parental feedback" as "criticism."

Next, Hanley asked school representatives how they would monitor the implementation of Elaine's IEP, how teachers would utilize resources provided by Don and Barb, and how the school would ensure adequate staff training.

A Long Record of Frustrations

Following the June 25 meeting, Lynn Hanley drafted a letter on July 11 to all members of the IEP team, this time providing a summary of the agreed-upon elements for Elaine's individualized education program. He noted that the team had reviewed the basics of aphasia (causes and effects), the characteristics specific to Elaine, her academic abilities, and her testing results. He also noted that Elaine tested consistently with an above average intelligence but suffered occasional shutdowns with subsequent depressions leading to withdrawal.

> Elaine's condition affects her ability to receive and send audio communications. It does not reflect her innate intelligence...OFTEN, Elaine's difficulty...precipitates a "shutdown" due to her stress from not readily recognizing audio communications from those people attempting to communicate to her...As a result, Elaine becomes depressed and withdrawn. This gives the appearance that she is uncooperative.

Hanley points out that he has referenced state and federal educational regulations throughout his letter.

His letter then reviews the Schultzes' specific requests, as recorded in the June 25 IEP meeting. Don and Barb had requested an audio-trainer device, which reduces ambient noise. This request conformed to Montana state law, according to Hanley. They had also requested that Elaine would use a "smart pen" or otherwise be allowed the use of a keyboard for completion of in-class assignments and homework. Handwriting was very laborious for Elaine. This "request," in fact, appeared as an agreement in the previous spring IEP meeting, but the school had nonetheless refused to comply, ignoring the fact an IEP has the authority of a legal contract.

Hanley then noted in his letter that Barb and Don had again reminded the IEP team of Elaine's need for visual aids in all of her subjects. Elaine needed more and better visual aids, and teachers needed education in how to create and use them. Hanley reminded them that Elaine "can perform capably when visual aids are used in all of her course work." Indeed, the school had routinely agreed to this, but had not implemented it.

The Schultzes had repeatedly asked that Elaine be given two weeks of lead time before her tests and quizzes. Elaine needed this time for preparation toward the testing process itself, not toward comprehension of the material. Elaine's tests and quizzes should also, as much as possible, be delivered in visual format so that her tests would accurately reflect her learning abilities. By delivering visual format tests, the teachers could also, to an extent, measure their effectiveness in instructing and testing a student with aphasia. Hanley carefully laid out all of this, building a case that Don, Barb, and their allies had thoroughly built before.

Hanley again expressed concerns about the turnover among Elaine's resource teachers and the lack of training among the new resource teachers regarding an aphasic student's needs. The problem of staff turnover deeply concerned Don and Barb, and Hanley addressed this issue at length in his letter.

> Starting in the 97-98 school year, Elaine will have been instructed by three resource teachers. The Schultzes are concerned that there is a learning curve of resource personnel dealing with aphasia and

that learning curve seems to be starting all over again with a newly hired or newly certified resource teacher.

Their concern encompassed not only MCS personnel, but staff at the Prickly Pear Special Services Cooperative also. Prickly Pear was not a part of MCS, but they worked very closely with the MCS administration, providing resource teachers and materials.

The issue of turnover among personnel involved a particular complication that felt uncomfortably revealing for the school. Hanley explained what may have been a conflict of interests, especially in the case of Terri Ortlund's dismissal:

> The Schultzes are concerned with the turnover in the administration of the Prickly Pear Special Services Cooperative…this turnover can only distract the cooperative from delivering relevant and efficient support to MCS. Although MCS does not exercise direct control of the cooperative, an MCS official sits on the PPSSC board. The Schutlzes feel the MCS trustee should advocate stability in administration of the cooperative and focus upon development and retention of PPSSC expertise in aphasia to better serve MCS and other client school districts.

This comment by Hanley, full of implications, did not sit well with Superintendent Willett or Principal Filmore.

The turnover among PPSSC resource teachers led to multi-layered, adverse consequences for Elaine and her parents, as well as for the school itself. The revolving door of resource teachers severely hampered school programs for disabled students. Training for MCS teachers dealing specifically with an aphasic student was non-existent. Whatever general training in disabilities and related pedagogy that took place for a PPSSC resource teacher was lost with her departure. Finally, the situation left Don and Barb themselves, as well as other parents, with the recurring and overwhelming task of providing the unwanted education for Elaine's teachers.

Through their attorney, Don and Barb also requested that in the next IEP meeting, they would meet with the current IEP team and previous team members as well. Perhaps they could thus involve Terri Ortlund one more time at least.

Elaine's fourth grade school year would begin soon, yet the MCS administration had not clearly confirmed what services and equipment they would provide. One brief note in Hanley's letter carried a painful sting: "Don and Barb insist that speech therapy in a hallway is not appropriate." Speech therapy had also involved Elaine being pulled out of class at odd times of day—and into the hallway with no resources at hand and where she felt embarrassingly exposed.

While MCS had again acknowledged the Schultzes' request that Wednesdays be set aside for accommodating Elaine's academic needs (via Sylvan, St. Peter's Hospital, and Sandi McGuire), the school had not yet granted that request. Hanley again raised the question. Would the school agree to release Elaine from MCS on Wednesdays and accept Sylvan instruction as an adequate substitute?

Given that the new school year was about to begin, Hanley asked who the new resource teacher would be. Would he or she have time for orientation and training, in anticipation of their work with Elaine?

On a conciliatory note, Hanley acknowledged several agreements reached by the IEP team in the meeting of June 25. Teachers and other MCS staff would respond more quickly to Elaine's need for her inhaler. Don and Barb would recommend resources and continue providing assistance, albeit more limited in scope. They and the teachers would routinely use a "traveling notebook"—that is, a logbook of what teachers had done with Elaine and of what concerns they had. This notebook served to facilitate a sharing of ideas from teacher to teacher and teacher to parent. The notebook also provided a partial means of monitoring how well the school implemented the terms of the IEP.

Through the traveling notebook and other reports from teachers, the school would provide clear documentation of Elaine's progress. Hanley assured the school and the Schultzes that he would "facilitate the anticipated cooperation for the parties to reasonably meet their duties and obligations," as defined by Montana educational and administrative regulations.

Agreements Without Follow-Through

While MCS officials had invited Don and Barb to provide helpful resources and had agreed, ostensibly, that parents should not have to reteach or excessively tutor their child, very little had changed in the school's implementation of Elaine's IEPs up to this point in time. IEP meetings continued, agreements were reached, discussions were repeated, and requests were resubmitted, yet all lead to increased frustration for Don and Barb.

On July 22, Hanley sent another letter to MCS, calling them out for their refusal to respond to his letter of July 11. He began by asking Principal Filmore and Superintendent Willett if they concurred with his summary of the June 25 meeting. He briefly reviewed key issues that the school had not yet addressed. "The 97-98 school year is rapidly approaching, and we need to know what services and equipment will be made available for Elaine and what training specific to Elaine's condition will be made available to her new resource teacher?" he wrote.

He then asked, "By the way, who is her new resource teacher?"

Next, he posed a question smoldering at the heart of the conflict. "I also wish to ask the more fundamental question of whether or not the Montana City School believes Elaine can perform better than she has supposedly demonstrated in the past?" If not, would they please review the evaluation provided by Dr. Annette McCormick and the progress reports provided by Sylvan Learning Center? If indeed MCS teachers and administrators believed that Elaine's LD status indicated that she could not improve, would they please provide and document a thorough evaluation proving so, as required by the school and state regulations?

Hanley understood clearly, as school administrators apparently did not, that merely providing a student's weak academic record, achieved in the absence of appropriate accommodations, did not constitute evidence that a student could not perform well if appropriately accommodated.

An Ambivalent Response

The director of the Montana Office of Public Instruction, Sarah Owens, responded to Hanley's letters, but not to Hanley himself. Instead, on July 23, she addressed a letter to Don and Barb. Indeed, Hanley would not receive a direct response from the OPI or the school until August 19.

Owens' letter to the Schultzes detailed her interpretation of the IDEA, school regulations, Elaine's IEP, and responsibilities of parents and school personnel. She acknowledged that the IEPs were "already signed off, so the issue is whether they are fully implemented." She also acknowledged Barb's concern regarding the teachers' failure to comply with two specific points in Elaine's IEP: in all classes the use of an auditory trainer (a microphone/speaker device that enhances the clarity of sound), and provision of visual cues for all assignments and tests.

In a somewhat conciliatory vein, Owens affirmed that MCS teachers must have specific skills developed in order to deliver free appropriate public education (FAPE) effectively to each student. Such skills could be "obtained through formal training, in-service, or consultation," she said. And while she agreed that the administration should provide structural support for teachers, she subtly shifted the weight of responsibility from the school to the parents: "Your district speech/language pathologist has information about aphasia. You may want to consult with her..." This was, ironically, the full extent of Owens' recommendation in response to Barb's insistence that MCS teachers needed substantially more education and training in how to deal properly with an aphasic student.

The OPI director's letter struck Don and Barb as condescending, contradictory, and evasive. For instance, she did not affirm the diagnosis provided by McCormick, but instead referred to it as Elaine's "suspected" disability. "The CST [Child Study Team] may want to review the area of suspected disability and plan for assessments, such as audiology or occupational therapy, in addition to the academic, and speech/language and intellectual assessments required."

Throughout what amounted to a defense of the school or a counterpoint to Don and Barb's concerns, Owens seemed implicitly to affirm the position taken by MCS officials—that no outside expertise would be accepted.

With a stunning irony, however, she informs Don and Barb that if they disagree with the school district's evaluation, they may "obtain an independent educational evaluation at private expense" and that "the results of the evaluation must be considered by the school district in any decision made with respect to the provision of a free appropriate public education" for Elaine. In other words, she ignored the fact that Don and Barb had already amassed and presented evidence and testimonials from multiple professional sources—not only the January 1997 evaluation from McCormick (clinical neuro-psychologist), but also assessments from Flynn (speech pathologist at the local hospital), McGuire (LPC therapist), Levesque (M.D.), Sylvan Learning Center instructors, and Terri Ortlund (previous resource teacher for MCS/PPSSC).

Even more confusingly, Owens then recommended that Don and Barb have Elaine comprehensively reevaluated yet again by the Child Study Team at Montana City School before the fall semester began. It was important, she said, to have an accurate assessment of Elaine's academic performance. Instead of acknowledging those external voices already provided, Owens merely pitted "your current assessment" against the previous assessment made by the school's own CST.

The Schultzes believed that this rejection of outside expertise and the repeated suggestion that they accept the MCS assessment created a conflict of interests. Who could properly diagnose Elaine, and in whose interest would the diagnosis be given? In confronting these questions, it troubled Don and Barb further that the school (and Prickly Pear Special Services) had already terminated a dissenting voice, Terri Ortlund.

The OPI director's letter was troubling on yet another point. Granting the problematic nature of scrutinizing someone's meaning and intent at this distance in time, it seems that Owens, in her letter to Barb, conflated two ideas: "performance" and "ability." First, she says this: "As I review the Child Study Team (CST) report you provided me, the abilities of your daughter described in the report and your current assessment of her abilities do not concur."

Then, as if a measure of innate abilities and a measure of performance at a specific point in time are the same, she says this: "...the key to an appropriate and successful educational program for you daughter lies in accurately describing her present level of performance...Administrative Rules (ARM) 10.16.1101 also requires school districts to assess the student's performance in curricular areas."

The confusion in Owen's language explains somewhat the apparent conflict of interest.

On the one hand, MCS officials seemed to believe that Elaine's "performance" in coursework, as measured by classroom tests and homework grades, corroborated the CST assessment results regarding her abilities. On the other hand, the CST evaluation of Elaine's innate abilities seemed inappropriately to rely on the same classroom test results and homework grades provided by Elaine's teachers. Both sets of results, in their estimation, confirmed that Elaine had reached her potential and could not learn at a pace or on a par with her classmates.

The OPI director ended her letter with another ironic statement: "If you believe that the current IEP is appropriate and that it is not being implemented as written, you may file a complaint with this office." Don and Barb hardly knew whether to take this as mere dismissiveness or as a gauntlet thrown. It felt like a taunt, in fact; their complaint had already reached the office of the OPI. In any case, surely by now they had made themselves clear.

CHAPTER 13

Pedagogies at Issue

Elaine learns best when presented with visuals and manipulatives that accompany verbal lessons. She can learn from text and voice, but what may stand for other students as a "strength" or "preference" in controversial learning styles parlance stood for Elaine as a primary and essential mode of knowledge acquisition. Elaine's aphasia significantly limited her ability to learn at a normal pace from text and speech alone without a highly visual (and tactile) pedagogy.

Since the publication of a meta-study in 2009, many researchers have insisted that there is no scientifically derived evidence that teaching to students' learning "styles" or "preferences" has any positive effect on their performance. On the other hand, it is a mistake to assess Elaine using the terms of that debate. Her birth injuries specifically target the language centers of her brain, producing her global aphasia—that is, her difficulty with language acquisition, comprehension, and expression.

Any teaching method that ignores the fact of her aphasia will meet with limited success, and her history of learning much more quickly and much better when visuals accompany verbal instruction is unambiguous. So long as she can prove her ability to learn—that is, demonstrate her learning on a par with other students by whatever means—she is "otherwise qualified" to participate in a mainstream educational setting, according to the law. She can learn, and she has—when teachers adjust their teaching methods in response to her aphasia.

Elaine's aphasia, along with the anxieties she had developed in her early school years, also presented a strenuous challenge to her mental and emotional endurance.

During her work with Elaine, Terri Ortlund had noticed Elaine's need for thoughtful pacing, as well as for periodic breaks. Wednesdays were Elaine's most difficult days and pressing Elaine beyond her endurance led to her "shutdowns." Terri routinely varied the rhythms and methods of her teaching, so that Elaine could avoid overload and continue learning, both more effectively and efficiently and without abnormal stresses. Terri had Elaine move around, use her hands, and learn with words and images together. The physical, tactile activities served the dual purpose of continuing her instruction and of relieving her stress. Terri's methods worked very well.

The OPI director, Sarah Owens resisted, nonetheless, and seemed relentless in her pursuit of a justification. In that letter to Barb, she took issue with the language of Elaine's IEP, for instance.

> The phrase "make use of visual cues" is also confusing. The types of visual cues you shared with me are instructional materials and methods. It is obvious that your family has put much effort into designing and providing these instructional materials. You also told me that you believe these instructional methods provide success for your daughter.

The director followed those observations with an explanation of why the school had set Barb's materials aside.

In doing so, however, Owens widely skirted the central questions in the conflict between the Schultzes and the school: Was Elaine thriving? If not, was the school properly accommodating Elaine's aphasia?

> Whether the school approaches the instruction of your daughter in the same manner [as Barb had urged] is a decision school personnel must make. If a particular type of instruction is the only

way to provide a free appropriate education (FAPE), it would be appropriate to include that method in the student's IEP.

Indeed, final decisions about how best to meet a student's needs belong to the school. If the pedagogy chosen by the school does in fact provide FAPE, then so be it. The astounding irony, however, is that school administrators and some teachers seemed to be arguing that Elaine could not succeed further, while yet dismissing substantial evidence that Elaine could advance if the school would alter their pedagogy.

Owens was also right in terms of what federal and state regulations required. The school had no obligation to fulfill the parents' wishes—that is, no obligation to do things the way a parent believes they should be done. She wrote, "In recent court cases where a school district's instructional method provides FAPE, even though the parent desires instruction through a different method, the school will have met its obligation under the IDEA."

Despite her accurate understanding of the law on that specific point, Owens failed to note an essential fact: MCS was not providing for Elaine with a reasonable and equal opportunity for success.

In terms of what constitutes an appropriate response to a student's disability support needs, Owens failed to acknowledge Elaine's proven innate abilities and likewise failed to provide accommodations designed to remedy the specific disadvantages posed by Elaine's aphasia. MCS had, over and over, proven to be inflexible in their teaching methods. And their teaching methods did not work for Elaine.

Sarah Owens took issue with yet another element of Elaine's IEP, creating further confusion about the status of an IEP, and in this case an IEP the director had clearly affirmed as "already signed off" by members of the Child Study Team.

The 1/28/97 IEP which you shared states: "Elaine will make use of augmentative devices such as auditory trainers and the AlphaSmart"...These statements may lead to confusion about your daughter's program needs and the services the school must provide. It is not clear whether your daughter requires the use of assistive technology such as an auditory trainer.

Owens insisted next that the Schultzes should seek an "assistive technology evaluation." She then provided them with a technical assistance manual and the necessary contact information within the Office of Public Instruction.

That raised frustrating questions for Don and Barb. Had the Child Study Team's (CST) signing off on Elaine's IEP confirmed Elaine's need for assistive technology or not? If the CST had made that confirmation, then why should the Schultzes need to reference the technical assistance manual and call the OPI education specialist (again)? By this time, in late summer of 1997, the Schultzes' frustrations had deepened, Elaine's stress had intensified, and they all approached the coming academic year with grave, unresolved concerns.

Several months later, not long after Don and Barb made the decision to pull Elaine from the Montana City School system, another OPI official confided in them. Had they kept Elaine in the school, she said, they would have had a solid case against the school in court. Elaine's school and medical records provided ample evidence, and Owen's letter unwittingly validated their most compelling arguments.

Barb Takes Aim

Barb penned two letters, dated July 31, one addressing a few familiar issues with Superintendent Willett and Principal Filmore, and the other answering OPI Director Sarah Owens. Barb reminded Willett and Filmore please to make Elaine's teachers and counselors aware of Elaine's need for an asthma inhaler. They must also follow the predetermined schedule for its use.

Barb noted again her concern about turnover among resource teachers.

Could Elaine and the new teacher get to know each other in time for the new teacher to help craft an optimal IEP before they progressed too deeply into the fall semester of fourth grade? What training would the new resource and the classroom teacher receive, regarding how to address the needs of an aphasic student?

Finally, Barb again asked that MCS release Elaine from the classroom each Wednesday. "It is well documented that Elaine shuts down by mid-week (Wednesday). We are proposing that Wednesdays be Elaine's appointment day." On Wednesdays, in other words, Elaine could attend the Sylvan Learning Center and also her speech therapy sessions with Sandi McGuire at St. Peter's Hospital. In both settings, Elaine felt calm, confident, and trusting in a one-on-one relationship with mentors, teachers, and therapists. In both settings, Elaine learned both quickly and well.

Of the many ironies and seeming contradictions in Sarah Owen's letter, this one stands out. She informed the Schultzes that, if an evaluation indicates that Elaine cannot achieve a goal "with supplemental aides and services in the regular classroom setting, then another placement should be identified." Did the director mean that a Wednesday away from the school might yet be possible, despite earlier claims that a release from class on Wednesdays would violate state and school regulations, or was she implying that Elaine might need a different placement entirely, away from the Montana City School?

Barb's letter to Owens had begun with a concession: "As per our conversation, I have requested a comprehensive educational evaluation for our child." However, Barb cut directly to the core contention next: "I realize that the school does not have to approach the instruction of our daughter in the same manner that we have presented. However, it is well documented by all involved in her instruction that it is a method which works well."

Barb did not need to repeat the obvious, the truth which both the Schultzes and MCS officials affirmed: Elaine was not thriving in the classroom. The ongoing battle revolved around the question of why.

A Final Push

Along with her letter, Barb had provided the OPI director and MCS staff and administrators with a packet of testimonial letters, descriptions of Elaine's learning processes, and practical examples of successful teaching methods, all confirming Elaine's abilities and disability. Barb titled the packet, "Celebrate Differences and Learning Together."

In an opening note for the packet, Don and Barb acknowledged that Elaine "is not the only child at Montana City School who is on an individual education program." They also acknowledged that as parents, they bore great responsibility for the "overall success" of their child. Nonetheless, they likewise asserted the obligations borne by the school: "Providing or creating an environment which enables each student, despite his or her 'handicap,' to succeed academically is the responsibility of the school."

Defiant inflexibility among MCS administrators and some teachers remained the norm, however, throughout the summer of 1997 and into Elaine's fourth grade year. The packet assembled by Don and Barb served as a launching point for their final attempts to break through that defiance. In the packet, they had assembled testimony from sources by then familiar to the school: Terri Ortlund, Rena Foley, and Alexis Flynn. Together, they again presented summary evidence that Elaine could learn and, in fact, did learn sufficiently well to keep pace with her classmates.

Also in their opening note, Don and Barb again conceded that Elaine was struggling. They had discovered that Elaine was not grasping "a great majority of the topics in the sciences as they were taught in school." They then addressed the "why" of Elaine's difficulty, reviewing a familiar list of issues: Elaine will become distracted by her environment, then impatient, and then disoriented when presented with too much verbal information. She learns best when working one-on-one. She tends to be quiet, but her facial expressions clearly indicate her emotional state. "It is essential to take cues from Elaine," the Schultzes explained, especially to note "if she is getting frustrated. If the instructor has developed a good working relationship with her, picking up the cues will not be a problem."

Barb and Don then provided a succinct explanation of Elaine's learning difficulties and abilities and suggested the best way to address them. "Elaine tests very poorly because most tests are verbally mediated. On the flip side, when Elaine is given tasks without a verbal component, she functions in the average to above average range. In fact, her visual memory abilities are in the superior range."

Next, they reviewed for the school their own successful methodology. Elaine wanted to learn how to cook, so at home, Don and Barb created visual instructions for making Elaine's favorite breakfast foods—French toast, for example. They also made a set of "kitchen rules" for measuring ingredients. Simple drawings of cooking utensils, pieces of toast, eggs, and a bottle of syrup accompanied the terms and instructions. Similar visuals often appear on boxed ingredients for many sorts of prepared foods

Barb and Don attempted an encouraging note, providing school personnel with further suggestions: "Teaching visually became fairly simple, as many of the basic concepts could be easily made visual through experiments and by observing things in nature," they explained. Using flashcards and conducting hands-on experiments also proved helpful for Elaine. Barb then described her success with such methods. "After I applied visual and hands-on instructing techniques in teaching, Elaine not only grasped many of the science concepts, but became enthusiastic in learning science."

Shoulder to Shoulder in the Push

Another contributor to the "Celebrate" packet, Elaine's speech pathologist from St. Peter's Hospital, Alexis Flynn, reinforced Barb and Don's claims. She advised school personnel to make regular use of visual aids—for example, drawings—to accompany words, especially drawings of people, as well as cartoon drawings and flow charts to illustrate the sequencing of ideas. Elaine grasped patterns. "Elaine's motivation to learn improved through this process, and minimal guidance was needed from the teacher," she wrote.

With a direct and concise assertion, Flynn advanced what was, at heart, a very simple concept with highly practicable applications: "Visual structure promotes learning for Elaine." Visual structures proved effective in teaching Elaine subject concepts and behaviors and in assessing Elaine's performance. Elaine consistently demonstrated mastery through her own drawings accompanying her written work. Indeed, Flynn noted Elaine's talent for drawing beautiful pictures that took a lot of time to produce. Elaine's perfectionism interfered in such work, so Flynn suggested that teachers might need to help Elaine complete her drawings more quickly.

Flynn's final suggestions recognized other specific elements of Elaine's learning patterns and processes. She urged teachers to look directly at Elaine when addressing her. The use of an FM system and an audio-trainer device would enhance the verbal information while Elaine focused on the images. And always seat Elaine away from distractions as much as possible.

Perhaps at considerable "political" risk to their appeal to school personnel, Don and Barb again invoked the help of Terri Ortlund, Elaine's beloved resource teacher from the first semester of her third grade. School administrators had ignored the Schultzes' pleading to see Terri rehired, but her insight and encouragement were invaluable. "Elaine is a very bright child," she wrote, "and once things are lodged in her brain, they stay there and will be remembered for years to come." Elaine "can be hard on herself," she added, and then implored MCS personnel to be encouraging and "sensitive to her ability to learn." Terri likewise strongly affirmed Elaine's artistic talent: "Her artistic ability is incredible."

For the teachers specifically, Terri Ortlund gave similar suggestions. "When things get tough, and you need to tell her something, draw it out for her or tell her to draw it for you." Be patient, she said, as "Elaine is getting so much better at verbally expressing herself." Terri further reminded the teachers that Elaine loved to study history, especially in the *World Magazine* and *National Geographic for Kids*.

Terri reaffirmed, for what must have seemed a hundredth time, Elaine's needs for accommodations specific to her aphasia and other health issues. Elaine needed help maintaining the correct schedule with her inhaler during the school day so that she could also stay on track with her evening doses at home. She needed an auditory trainer device during class sessions. She must be taught in a visual way. Terri acknowledged that "this requires a lot of work from all involved…but this is how Elaine learns." Elaine needed a two-week notice before each test. That prior notice also served those preparing her tests, as they must remember that visual prompts for test answers were most effective.

Lastly, and in more detail, Terri addressed the issue of Elaine shutting down under too much verbal information and of her need for Wednesdays away from class at MCS. "What you need to look for," she wrote,

> are times and periods where things are the most stressful for Elaine. The middle of the week (Wednesday) in particular seems to be the roughest day. Wednesdays would be an opportune time to do life-skills, like cooking, sewing, or keyboarding…She would benefit in many ways by the use of computers for visual learning, including the use of Alpha-Smart pen, as handwriting is very strenuous for her.

Alexis Flynn, Terri, Don, and Barb had again done what they could to provide evidence and testimony on Elaine's behalf. The "Celebrate" packet represented for them a few essential things: great confidence in Elaine, a waning hope that MCS would respond appropriately, and a careful step forward in the legal battle surrounding Elaine.

CHAPTER 14

Summer Ends In Exhaustion

A Dispute with the Attorney

On August 19, shortly before the new school year began, Superintendent Willett finally sent a letter to the Schultzes' attorney, Lynn Hanley. She acknowledged receipt of his summary of the June 25 IEP meeting but referred to the meeting date as June 11. She also acknowledged receipt of the "Celebrate" packet from Don and Barb. She then identified Elaine's new "case manager" and "resource teacher," claiming that Elaine was already familiar with her.

Item by item, she then addressed Hanley's summary of that late-June IEP meeting, sharply disputing the accuracy of the attorney's memory. "The itemized 'understandings' discussed in your letter of June 11, 1997 do not accurately reflect our discussion."

First, she acknowledged the Schultzes' request for an auditory trainer and an Alpha-Smart Pen, but failed to address the complaint from Don, Barb, and their attorney that MCS had not followed through by securing those assistive devices. Second, she recognized that Elaine was, indeed, a visual learner and assured the attorney that future IEP meetings will address this point.

On the third item from the attorney's letter, Superintendent Willett betrayed a stubborn misunderstanding. She insisted that the teachers' mode of testing Elaine (mentioning specifically multiple-choice questions) were adequate, "if material was previously taught visually." Thus, she ignored Elaine's need for visual prompting of recall during tests. She also rejected the request for a two-week prior notice for tests because "material is not always studied for that period of time." Her response ignored Elaine's specific challenges and needs as distinct from the needs of other students.

Offering more of what felt like evasion and persistent misunderstanding, Willett affirmed that she and the school principal would "continue to facilitate training" of personnel to enhance their understanding of aphasia and of how best to teach Elaine. The word "continue" struck Hanley and the Schultzes as ironic. Such training had not yet occurred in any systematic or substantive manner, the request for such training was long-standing, and the new school year would begin within days. Furthermore, she offered no details or plan for the training other than to cite Terri Ortlund's and Mrs. Smith's brief visits to the School for Deaf and Blind and to Montana State University during the previous year.

Responding to Hanley's next summary item, Willett expressed resentment over the insinuation that the administrative connections between MCS and Prickly Pear Special Services Cooperative might involve a conflict of interests. The new director of PPSSC was, she said, the ex-director of the Montana Office of Public Instruction. That fact did not comfort the Schultzes or their attorney. The previous OPI director had demonstrated neither sympathy for Elaine nor a clear understanding of the school's obligations.

Perhaps in a conciliatory effort, Willett claimed that MCS personnel "are in no way asking the Schultzes to be more than a member of the team." This claim left Don and Barb especially frustrated. Barb recalls how she and Don felt compelled to reteach nearly everything to Elaine virtually every day after school. Over and over, they had informed MCS of their extraordinary efforts in the evenings and on weekends. They had also provided MCS with massive proof that in a quiet environment and with the correct teaching methods, Elaine could learn on a pace with her classmates. In her letter to attorney Hanley, however, Willett again rejected evidence from experts outside of the school, which specifically cited Elaine's performance records from the non-MCS summer programs in which Elaine had participated.

The Willett's letter concluded with a false assertion that Hanley had raised "several new concerns" in his summary of the June 25 IEP meeting (which she again referred to as the June 11 meeting). "In addition," she wrote, "changes to Elaine's program for the school year are indicated that have never been a part of our discussion or an IEP." She cited the request for Wednesday's off as an example, despite the appearance of that request on previous IEPs and in previous letter exchanges between the Schultzes, Terri Ortlund, other professionals, and the school.

And a Dispute with the Schultzes

On August 19, Superintendent Willett sent a letter to Don and Barb as well. The letter parallels, for the most part, the letter she sent to Hanley on the same day. Her letter to the Schultzes did not carry the same caustic tone as did her letter to their attorney, but one cannot call her letter conciliatory either. She indicated that the "Celebrate" packet had reached her and that she would ask the school principal, teachers, and staff to review it and share ideas. She also quoted a short paragraph in which Hanley describes Elaine as "afflicted with aphasia."

For the Schultzes, as for many in the disability community, such words as "afflicted," "wheelchair-bound," "bedridden," or "suffer" stir up ambivalence and raise a particular concern. Those words do convey a genuine and appreciated sympathy of course. On the other hand, words that emphasize the affliction and suffering of a person with disability may also express unwanted pity and contribute to misunderstanding by overdramatizing the challenges that someone faces. In the context of a conflict over whether a school administration is meeting a student's needs, expressions of pity may subtly deflect from the problem of inadequate accommodations and imply that someone needs a level of care a school cannot provide.

What Elaine needed, and what Don and Barb wanted for her, was an emphasis on her abilities. Indeed, Elaine faced a complex challenge with her aphasia; she faced an obstinate obstacle, however, among some of her MCS educators, and her hope for a sense of normalcy suffered a blow.

Beyond that single reassurance and the ambivalent expression of sympathy, Willett merely quoted passages from the attorney's letter, acknowledging the IEP terms requested by the Schultzes, yet providing neither affirmation that teachers would follow through nor guidance for implementation if they did. Yes, the Schultzes had requested the use of auditory trainers "in all of [Elaine's] classes, not just science and math." Yes, they had requested an Alpha-Smart Pen or laptop for Elaine. Yes, they believed that she needed a visual pedagogy from teachers trained in that approach.

Don and Barb again confronted an old irony in this letter from the superintendent. She remained non-committal toward the acknowledged requests yet confirmed again that Elaine's IEPs were already signed off by members of the IEP team. "Other items discussed during the June 11, 1997 meeting" (which in fact took place on June 25) "that I believe are important in the consideration of Elaine's program for the 1997-1998 year are" in the current IEP, she wrote. And the remainder of her letter involved a series of denials, rejections, and misunderstandings.

No, MCS could not release Elaine from classes on Wednesdays, nor could they release her from the final hour of class each day. Willett then cited a state regulation: "It is the responsibility of her parents to cause her to attend school." She offered no authoritative decision and suggested no resolution regarding Elaine's speech therapy taking place in a hallway or in the middle of a test. Regarding multiple-choice tests, she argued that, while Elaine "cannot write an essay...yes, she can draw and label." Once again, she missed the point that Elaine needed visual prompts accompanying her test questions and that, in fact, she could write an essay when visually prompted. She repeated her rejection of a two-week prior notice before tests, arguing that "material is not always studied for that period of time."

Superintendent Willett turned her attention next to the vexing issue of turnover among resource teachers. She repeats her ironic promise that

MCS "has and will continue to facilitate" the adequate training of teachers regarding aphasia and visual teaching. She then added, "I hope that we can all understand that Elaine will have teachers that are new to her each year and each teacher and team member will have to work to learn about Elaine's special needs."

She then denied the Schultze's request for a teacher's aide, claiming falsely that the IEP team had not previously requested one and indicating that the new resource teacher would be available Monday through Friday.

She did agree that the traveling notebooks had worked well for Elaine, her parents, and her teachers throughout third grade, but unsettled that issue by insisting that "expectations for using this system need to be discussed and agreed upon by the team." Don and Barb had received no previous indication that the traveling notebooks were problematic. Nonetheless, Willett wanted clarification about who should be given copies of lesson plans, how much homework Elaine should have, and who would review her daily work. Those things had been established, or so thought Don and Barb.

In any case, Sarah Willett's letter again raised a perplexing question: Why had she delayed for so long her response to the attorney and to the Schultzes? What could the IEP team accomplish in time for Elaine to benefit fully at semester start-up? She noted the Schultzes' request for a full reevaluation of Elaine and suggested that the IEP team might consider "extending the IEP that is in place" through the "comprehensive evaluation period." The team could then write a new IEP, she argued, the deadline for which was September 17, less than a month away. Teachers and administrators had largely ignored the old IEP; and now a new one would come late.

Wrapping up her response to Don and Barb, Willett insisted that MCS was, in fact, meeting their obligation to provide free appropriate public education (FAPE).

CHAPTER 15

A Year Begins...to Crumble

By the end of summer after Elaine's third grade year, the frequent but fruitless IEP meetings with teachers, counselors, and administrators had grown exhausting and exasperating. They had led to no clear plan, no definitive actions, and no positive results for Elaine. The school administration seemed impervious to appeals, no matter who voiced them, whether personal or professional. Late letters from the superintendent, delivering mostly evasion and denial, further subverted hopes for resolution and progress.

Don and Barb forged ahead with that combination of frustration, skepticism, and weariness that defines a protracted hope. They had done their homework, fought these battles before, and learned how difficult and exhausting the fight could be.

What Must Be

On the one hand, a school does not face an obligation to please the parents of a student, and disagreements do not necessarily resolve in favor of parental wishes. Parents of students with disabilities sometimes educate themselves substantially regarding their state and local school regulations and educational processes, federal disability law, and the nature and impact of their children's disabilities. Still, parents often overreach, perhaps from overzealousness or from a weak understanding of what they read. They may confuse "equal access" (what schools must provide by law) and "success" (what only the student can achieve, or not, once equal access has been provided).

School officials may likewise pursue a professional understanding of disability law, of best practices for pedagogy and accommodation, and of the disabilities that students bring with them. Disagreements with parents do not necessarily resolve in favor of a teacher's or school administrator's wishes, however. School administrations tend to focus too narrowly on a set of legitimate institutional concerns: teacher workload, expense of personnel training, expense of disability-related resources and accommodations, and, thus, on meeting the minimum legal requirements.

What the law requires is that all parties involved in the educational process maintain a singular focus: what best serves the educational interests of the student. Protecting the integrity of an educational program is an essential part of that. Protecting the mental and emotional health of the student is likewise an essential part of that singular focus. Providing FAPE for an "otherwise qualified" student with disabilities is the essence of the legal obligations.

And What Was

Don and Barb indeed did their homework. They built their case. They sought help from Sandi McGuire, a private licensed professional counselor, and the pediatric psychologist, Dr. John Levesque. In an August 22, 1997 note to Levesque and shared with the Schultzes, Sandi described Elaine's "feelings of anger and insecurity, largely related to her aphasia and resulting academic difficulties." She cited Dr. Annette McCormick's psychological report from January of that year, agreeing with McCormick that Elaine suffered "shutdowns...when overwhelmed by verbal information." She also supported the Schultzes' "request to reduce the amount of time Elaine spends at school." Two weeks later, on September 5, Dr.

Levesque would send a letter to the MCS administrators recommending again a mid-week break for Elaine, or at least permission "to attend only core classes," thus freeing her to receive speech therapy at the hospital and instruction at Sylvan.

Armed with that letter from Sandi McGuire and the abundance of documentation from previous medical, psychological, and academic reports, Barb wrote another letter to the Montana City School officials, dated August 25. This letter focused primarily on the question of whether Elaine would spend her Wednesdays at the school or elsewhere. Barb reminded the IEP team that "the school environment becomes for her overwhelming and chaotic," and that "it is well documented that Elaine does shut down by mid-week. She becomes verbally overloaded, stressed, and frustrated by all 'the noise' (all the talking), what she perceives to be chaos."

Barb then explained to the team that "Elaine would not be at home on Wednesdays"; rather, she would be at the Sylvan Learning Center for reading, math, and writing instruction, and with Alexis Flynn, a speech therapist at St. Peter's hospital. Both places were structured, quiet, one-on-one learning environments, where Elaine could relax, regroup, and reinforce her MCS classroom learning.

A letter from Alice Frederics, a new Sylvan director, to the Montana City School, dated September 3, 1997, would confirm that, on August 27, Elaine had begun sessions at Sylvan and would continue each Wednesday after. On September 8, Alexis Flynn would notify MCS that Elaine had begun receiving "language service" at St. Peter's hospital.

The school's refusal to grant permission for Elaine's absence on Wednesdays (or otherwise early each day) rankled Don and Barb. In fact, the school had allowed a compromise before, as Barb reminded the school administrators in her letter: "At that time (last spring, with Elaine off early on Mondays to see a psychologist and two times each week with Alexis Flynn) no objections were voiced concerning our daughter's reduced hours at school."

Barb's next move was to inform the school officials that Elaine would, in fact, be gone on Wednesdays in order to work at Sylvan and at the hospital "as arranged." Barb then challenged the team to justify their refusal to give Elaine permission for those Wednesdays off. "In light of past experience, we request that the IEP team members voting against this request will support their decision with objective rationale and facts supporting their decision."

In her letter, Barb addressed a few other issues, long grown wearisome. She asked that the team periodically review and reevaluate Elaine's IEP on specified dates throughout the year. She repeated her earlier request for a teacher aide, despite the team's insistence that an aide would be inappropriate because Elaine might become dependent. That constituted an irrelevant and, therefore, legally indefensible objection. Either Elaine needed the help of a teacher aide, or she did not.

Furthermore, when either the classroom teacher or the resource teacher was absent, Barb had to fill in. That combined with the routine reteaching that she and Don did at home and the added expense of Elaine's work at Sylvan and the hospital indicated to Barb and Don that the school, in fact, did not provide FAPE, a free appropriate public education. Despite denial of permission from the school, Elaine had begun her schedule of Wednesdays off campus.

Finally, Barb raised again the issue of appropriate training for Elaine's teachers, counselors, and any others involved in her instruction. "We further assume that the PPSSC and MCS will identify and commit to particular, specialized, and timely training (regarding aphasia) for staff members having frequent contact with Elaine."

Three days after Barb sent her letter, Don sent his own appeal to the school principal, with a grievance stemming from a startling revelation. "We feel that Barb and I are the only remaining members of Elaine's IEP team and the only ones who know what teaching methods Elaine gains the most from." He continued with this stinging reminder: "A few months ago when I asked, you could not provide a definition for Elaine's condition; therefore, in my opinion, I cannot consider you as an informed IEP team member."

Don also expressed frustration at having to restate their many concerns, including "a lack of continuity in Elaine's education and instructional methods which were ineffective before but are going to be tried again." They had repeatedly asked the classroom teacher, without success, to employ teaching methods that Alexis Flynn used with great success at the hospital.

Hitting the Wall, Again

Despite renewed appeals from the Schultzes and additional documentation from outside experts, the school moved forward along the same unaltered track it had followed before. Barb recalls that once again, the speech pathologist pulled Elaine out of class in the middle of a test and conducted her speech therapy session in the hallway, leaving Elaine to finish her test at the end of the day. Elaine's teachers mostly refused to produce or provide visual aids for their lessons and yet again expressed resentment toward Barb for providing visuals of her own. The teachers generally refused to use them.

Elaine's two classroom teachers offered some encouragement and cooperated on some measures, at least briefly. In her traveling notebook entries for August 28, one teacher agreed to deliver clear instructions, specifically with Elaine in mind, and to provide a quiet place when Elaine became overwhelmed. She affirmed, too, that Elaine did well in science when outdoors making sensory observations. Furthermore, Elaine displayed confidence in volunteering to work at the blackboard, in one instance boldly locating Arizona on a map and speaking to the kids and the adults in the room. The teacher also asked to borrow Barb's sign language book, hoping to learn enough for more effective communication with Elaine.

Elaine's vocabulary instructor also noted that Elaine could effectively use her own drawings as illustrations for many geographical terms, and thus confirm her understanding. Traveling notebook entries from Elaine's other classroom teacher, dated September 2 and 4, indicated that Elaine was using cartoon drawings effectively in her creative writing assignments, which she completed at her own pace.

While the teacher believed that Elaine needed to function more independently, she nonetheless confirmed that Elaine did work well without assistance and demonstrated good organizational skills.

In her own entries from late August, as response to those from Elaine's teachers, Barb affirmed the value of the traveling notebook. The teachers' entries confirmed Elaine's participation in class and her comfort with familiar subjects. From the earliest days in the semester, however, Barb noted old, recurring problems. Thus, Barb requested copies of vocabulary cards for Elaine to review at home.

As she had in the past, Barb again expressed concern about Elaine's tendency to watch the other students for cues about what to do. That tendency became counterproductive, Barb argued, as an indication that Elaine was not fully understanding instructions on her own. Her teachers continued their habit of delivering instructions verbally, seldom with visual aids to accompany the flow of words.

Barb also wrote a notebook entry explaining that Elaine was already shutting down during math, a subject she favored. The school year had barely begun. The Schultzes and other parents objected to the Math Land program for a variety of reasons, but for Elaine, "the noise and energy level necessary for this program are too overwhelming," Barb asserted. She requested that Elaine therefore be pulled out of the regular math time and given a book.

Dr. McCormick Weighs in Again

At Don and Barb's request, Dr. Annette McCormick sent a letter to them, on September 2 of 1997, which they could in turn show to MCS officials. As Don had done in in June and August letters, McCormick took a direct, forceful approach:

Elaine's needs and what can be done to help her seem so clear that I find myself wondering why I am writing this letter. In our conversations, I am continually struck by the lack of cooperation/understanding between the school and the outside team (including Don and you [Barb]) working with Elaine.

McCormick then urged the team of parents and educators to engage in some team building for the sake of trust and effective communication.

With important implications for the school, McCormick further suggested that Don and Barb decrease the amount of "time they are intensively working with Laney" and increase time spent playing and relaxing with her. "Laney interprets intensive instructional time as expectations and works relentlessly" to please her parents. "At most," McCormick cautioned, "she should spend one hour per school day and two hours per weekend day involved in extra tutoring, etc."

The school must pick up the slack, in other words. McCormick then concurred with the pediatrician's recommendation that Elaine work within a shorter school day or shorter week. "I am in strong support of a break during Elaine's week, during which she can receive additional services. Such a break would also allow her to 'regroup.'"

McCormick ended her letter with a note that she had heard nothing from MCS administrators or teachers in response to her earlier attempts at communicating with them. By this time, the Schultzes' attorney had received a letter from the school, but hardly in time for any further action the school might take in preparation for Elaine's entry into fourth grade. McCormick never did get a response.

CHAPTER 16

IE...Procrastination

Time Is Running Out

Early in September of 1997, Don and Barb, their attorney Lynn Hanley, Alexis Flynn, and Sandi McGuire met with Elaine's primary classroom teacher in preparation for the upcoming IEP meeting set for September 17. This preliminary meeting gave the Schultzes and key supporters an opportunity to strategize. Elaine had already begun classes, but her schoolteachers and administrators had still not formulated a coherent, consistent, suitable plan for Elaine.

Hanley wrote a letter to Principal Filmore, laying out the essential rationale for Don and Barb's persistence in seeking appropriate accommodations for Elaine. He reminded the school officials that neither the Schultzes' requests nor the professional corroboration they had amassed was new. Furthermore, the testimony from professionals should indeed carry great force in the IEP team's deliberations.

> The opinions of treating physicians are so inherently valid that, in the absence of qualified and relevant opinions to the contrary (by other professionals with like familiarity and experience with Elaine Schultz), the recommendations of treating physicians are dispositive of what is best for their patient.

Hanley followed with an appeal to common sense: "Let's decide we can be *flexible*, while offering MCS control appropriate to its statutory responsibility to Elaine."

While Hanley could not claim correctly that a school is obligated to do everything that doctors recommend or do things in exactly the way they recommend, he was correct to assert the influence that outside professionals should have in an IEP team's deliberations. The school faced an obligation to recognize Elaine's disability, understand the nature and effects of that disability, and devise accommodations that provided Elaine with a fair and equal opportunity for success. While Hanley acknowledged the dual imperatives of providing Elaine with appropriate accommodations and yet protecting the integrity of their instructional program, he, the Schultzes, and their allies within and outside of MCS believed that the school had consistently failed to meet its legal obligations.

Elaine had so far failed to thrive. That alone did not prove she was not "otherwise qualified" to learn alongside her classmates at MCS. Evaluations by multiple professionals, proven success in non-MCS contexts, and repeated demonstrations that certain teaching methods worked very well for her constituted strong evidence that she was, in fact, capable and thus "otherwise qualified." Still, as before, the school administrators balked at most of the Schultzes' requests.

Befuddlements and Belated Responses

A few weeks after the IEP meeting of September 17, on October 1, attorney Hanley crafted another letter to the school principal. Point by point, his letter revealed the impasse facing Don and Barb. He asked Filmore for specific responses to recommendations from McCormick, Levesque, and McGuire. He also asked her to "provide the rationale for those responses." MCS had provided only minor and inconsistent accommodations, he recalled for her, and had again refused to acknowledge Elaine's absence on Wednesdays as acceptable.

Hanley rejected the notion, expressed by some at MCS, that the Schultzes' requests for accommodations had come as a surprise. "I cannot believe Elaine's needs have taken Montana City School by surprise. She has been a MCS student for years. The Schultzes are vocal advocates for their child. Yet we are into October with no firm game plan for Elaine."

Somewhat caustically, yet within reason, Hanley suggested that the school might use its resources more effectively for accommodations rather than for legal dispute resolution. "Montana City School is obligated to provide for Elaine" with resources "reflected in the MCS budget," and time was running out, he said.

Ironically, given earlier claims that compromise of the school schedule was prohibited by state and school regulations, the IEP committee did approve of an alternative to Wednesdays off. Elaine could leave school one hour early each day. This inconsistency puzzled Don, Barb, and their attorney, but they rejected that alternative as impractical and meaningless. Given their need to pick up Elaine's sister from school at the regular time, such a brief release at the end of the day would not allow Elaine to benefit from off-campus services at Sylvan or the hospital. Nor would such a brief release at day's end relieve Elaine from the day-by-day accumulation of stresses that led to her shutdowns.

The Schultzes and their attorney knew the relevant laws and regulations and did their best to leverage them.

> In the event a Wednesday pull-out is unacceptable to MCS, I remain unadvised of the reason. Is the current pull-out counting against Elaine, and in what way? Please include the rationale for the school's position…In light of statutory language acknowledging that other resources can be incorporated into an elementary school curriculum and given the fact that the Schultzes are more than willing to pay their fair share (perhaps more than) to obtain those services, I am at a loss to understand Montana City School's reluctance.

He and the Schultzes also knew of other students around the country whose accommodations included alternative placements. They knew something else, too, that they could not disclose to the IEP team without violating another student's privacy. Another patient of Dr. McCormick's attended classes at MCS through only half of each day.

Lynn Hanley addressed another issue as well. Why had the school refused to secure a teacher's aide for Elaine's teachers, even if only part-time? Why had they refused to consider an alternative to finding a teacher's aide from among their own staff? The Schultzes had contacts and had offered help with this, only to face rebuff.

The first response from the school, regarding the September 17 IEP meeting, came from the classroom teacher. She asked for a meeting with Don and Barb so that the three of them could discuss establishing suitable hours and settings for Elaine's special education services. She indicated that the next full IEP team meeting could not occur until October 10 or even 20. This communication from the teacher served more to frustrate than to encourage.

In a letter to Hanley, Barb vented some frustration over why the school only now seemed interested in discussing these issues. Why also had they for so long delayed responses to both Hanley and McCormick? Still galling to Don and Barb was the fact that, while the school had so stubbornly refused Wednesdays off for Elaine, they had seen fit to pull her from the middle of a math test for the sake of speech therapy in the hallway.

Toward Yet Another IEP

Members of the IEP team, including Barb and Don, agreed upon October 10 as the date for the next meeting. In preparing for that, Hanley informed Principal Filmore that he would accompany the Schultzes at the meeting. He provided some preliminary information and asked for more information from the school. "At this point, it would be very helpful if you would send copies to me of all communications made to the

Schultzes or any other professionals or individuals involved with Elaine or who may be part of the IEP process."

For the IEP team's benefit, he provided a letter from Dr. Levesque, the pediatric psychologist, and from Rena Foley, one of Elaine's Sylvan instructors.

Dr. Levesque suggested an alternative to Wednesdays off for Elaine. Perhaps the school could release Elaine from school after just four hours of attendance each day? Foley offered an implicit yet pointed rebuke to MCS officials. Elaine did very well with socialization at Sylvan. "She knows that she belongs and is accepted with the other children." She also demonstrated very strong progress academically in the absence of excessive verbal instruction and constant classroom noise. Those adverse conditions "are not present" at the Sylvan Learning Center, asserted Foley.

Along with his letter and those from Levesque and Foley, Hanley included a packet of testimonials from friends of the Schultzes. Each letter provided a strong character reference for Don and Barb and a clear affirmation of Elaine's intellectual and social abilities. Don and Barb had gathered these letters from friends, a coach, and a teacher, with some from Arizona, Illinois, and Montana. Even the parents of Nick, Elaine's beloved friend from her early school days in Illinois, contributed a letter.

An Ultimatum

On the day after the IEP meeting of October 10, Barb and Don issued an ultimatum. They would not sign the IEP until the school satisfactorily answered their questions about the vague goals stated in the IEP. Would Elaine's teachers make proper use of an audio-trainer for all verbal group activities, not only while the teacher was speaking? Had teachers or other staff members formulated a plan for helping Elaine through her most stressful periods and shutdowns? How would teachers and staff members follow through on their intention, stated in the IEP, to assess Elaine's communication and needs, in contexts outside of the classroom (playground or lunchroom, for instance)?

Once again, Dr. McCormick added her voice to the discussion. In an October 13 letter to the school Principal Filmore, who had previously expressed concern that McCormick "misperceived" the level of cooperation from MCS, McCormick offered an encouraging assessment of Elaine. After again reviewing all of the documentation that the Schultzes had provided, she felt impressed by and supportive of the creative and flexible pedagogy that Don and Barb had designed for their own use with Elaine. She also affirmed that she had "no concerns regarding Elaine's socialization, should she attend only a half day at school."

Far Too Little, Far Too Late

In early November, Don and Barb received an email from a teacher detailing her excitement over Elaine's joys and successes and explaining her efforts to accommodate Elaine. What prompted that teacher to respond with an uncharacteristic level of sympathy and eagerness remains unclear. Her response came too late. Referring to Elaine's first Wednesday back in the regular classroom, the teacher wrote, "Our first Wednesday! I hope it went well for Elaine." According to the teacher, "Elaine expressed great pleasure 'picturing' music," and "it was so relaxing she almost fell asleep."

The teacher continued by explaining her efforts to keep the other kids quiet when Elaine was in the classroom, while also being careful not to single out Elaine too much. The other kids understood Elaine very well, she said, as one "who learns different," but was "really, really smart." Barb and Don might have found such language encouraging, had it not come so late in an increasingly stressful semester and after several semesters fraught with tension.

CHAPTER 17

Crash

One month after the email to Don and Barb from Elaine's fourth grade classroom teacher, Elaine crashed.

On Friday, December 5, 1997, Elaine and her sister Anna got up for school as usual. Barb immediately noticed Elaine's unusual state of mind and odd behaviors. Barb felt alarmed. Seeming disoriented and lethargic, anxious and depressed, Elaine struggled with the simplest cognitive tasks—how to brush her teeth, dress, eat her breakfast, and gather her school supplies. She seemed muted, disoriented, and confused.

Elaine remembers the incident as disorienting and stunning for her and terrifying for her mother.

About halfway through grade four, I got up one morning, saying I don't know who my teacher is and asking who everyone was around me. I was basically done with everything. Almost like a black shade of color in my brain. I was absolutely done with school and those around me. I didn't go to class, and my mom took me to a clinic and then to the hospital.

On the morning of that severe shutdown, Barb rushed Elaine to Sandi McGuire, an education specialist and psychologist, who quickly recognized "that something significant was going on."

Elaine's description of her own state of mind deeply alarmed Sandi.

"*My mind is black...My brain hurts a lot,*" Elaine said. She described severe, persistent headaches and remembers feeling "*like I didn't know anything. I didn't know who anyone was. I wasn't even sure who I was.*" Barb and Sandi both remember saying, "We're losing her."

Sandi urged Barb to make an appointment with Dr. Levesque next, who agreed to see Elaine that day. Levesque noticed her confusion and profound memory loss first. She did not know her own age, the name of her school, her home address or phone number, or the names of her teachers or classmates. Elaine could not identify where she was at that moment.

Elaine's confusion and distress continued through Friday and worsened on Saturday. Levesque sent the Schultzes to the hospital in Great Falls, where Dr. Wight, a pediatric neurologist, could administer a CT, an EEG, an MRI, a spinal tap, and blood tests. With those tests completed, Barb and Don took Elaine back to Helena and home and waited for the test results.

Elaine's condition deteriorated further through late Saturday. She began vomiting at about 1:00 a.m. on Sunday, which she continued through that morning. Barb made a frantic call to Dr. Levesque, who admitted Elaine to the hospital early Sunday morning. Once they had Elaine settled in, Levesque ordered blood tests and drug screens. As her condition worsened, he ordered an emergency EEG and CAT Scan (test results from Wight had not yet come). The hospital nurses monitored Elaine throughout Sunday and reported that Elaine had shown some improvement by that afternoon and felt somewhat better by Monday morning. Despite her improving condition, Elaine continued to suffer periods of confusion throughout Monday and Tuesday. Finally, by Wednesday morning, Elaine felt close to normal.

Not everything had gone well at the hospital, as one pediatrician added another episode to Elaine's saga of frustrating encounters with inattention and ignorance, not only among some educators but also among some medical professionals. After making a cursory examination, the pediatrician expressed an unsympathetic befuddlement and brusquely admitted that he knew nothing about aphasia. "So I kicked him out of the room," Barb says, "and told him he was to have no more contact with Elaine." Barb laughs about that encounter now, even as her old indignation easily resurfaces.

Dr. Wight's test results arrived at the hospital in Helena on Monday, December 8, where Levesque reviewed test the results from his own and Wight's testing. Next, he consulted with Wight by phone. The imaging tests revealed some slight brain abnormalities that often accompany seizures, but they did not indicate that a seizure had occurred. The other test results all came back normal, providing no direct medical cause for Elaine's distress. Wight and Levesque both recorded Elaine's diagnosis as "a psychological response to adverse stimuli" at school—a shutdown, albeit a devastating instance far more severe than Elaine had experienced before.

What to Do About School

On Wednesday, December 10, Don wrote a letter to Elaine's IEP team. He reviewed the details of Elaine's shutdown on the previous Friday, the results of testing at the hospital, and the diagnosis that McGuire, Levesque, and Wight had agreed upon. Don described the extraordinary severity of this latest shutdown and informed the team that Elaine would resume attendance at school "in a slow and gradual manner…next week and for mornings only." He also told them that "all testing during this week prior to Christmas break needs to be suspended until after the new year. We want to prevent undue stress."

Barb's report the following summer to the Arizona DES conveyed the distress she had felt the year before, as well as Elaine's. Given the recalcitrance of MCS teachers and administrators, wrote Barb, she and Don could not sustain the heavy demands both of parenting and of reteaching Elaine. Barb had hoped to find a job but entering the job market "was not ever a remote possibility." She and Don had tried again to negotiate with MCS. "We did meet with the school to try and ease Elaine back into school. This was most unsuccessful. The resource teacher and classroom teacher would not heed the advice that the professionals were giving."

Nothing changed. No one at MCS budged. Elaine suffered. "Throughout the week, we felt our daughter slipping away from us."

The Schultzes had decided to make a dramatic change, Barb explained. "On December 18, we met with Sandi McGuire. She stated to both Don and me that she could not make Elaine whole in an hour each week and that, over Christmas break, we should consider homeschooling." After seeing Elaine at the clinic and following Elaine's progress over the next two weeks, Sandi had called the Schultzes, offering some bold, emphatic advice she had never before given any parents. In fact, as Sandi says now, "El was the only patient-student on behalf of whom I ever said, before or after this incident, 'You must homeschool your child. She's not getting what she needs at MCS.'"

That advice struck home, especially as they remembered Terri Ortlund's insistence that the school's neglect of Elaine constituted abuse. "Elaine's need first was to heal," Sandi had told them, and suggested that her role now should be to help Elaine and the family deal with the emotional and psychological impact of her experience at MCS. "Elaine at this time was extremely depressed and very withdrawn," said Barb, "We made the decision that evening that we would homeschool Elaine."

When Late Is Not Better Than Never

One of Elaine's classroom teachers sent a note of sympathy to Don and Barb on December 8, three days after Elaine's devastating shutdown. "Tell Elaine to relax," she wrote, "and tell her that she has a spelling test coupon for a free 100%. Let her know, too, that the other kids made cards for her." The teacher then suggested to Don and Barb that they hold Elaine out of school until Elaine's other classroom teacher could return from jury duty. The substitute teacher did not know Elaine, she said, and "could not do a good job." Two days later, the teacher sent an email, asking the Schultzes if they had "any news this evening" about Elaine's recovery. Her concern was noted and appreciated.

Not until December 22 did Don and Barb hear from Elaine's other classroom teacher, in response to news that Elaine would no longer attend MCS. Although somewhat sympathetic, the letter left Barb and Don feeling exasperated once again. The teacher gave a detailed narration of her work with Elaine on a Wednesday, nearly two weeks following her dramatic shutdown. To Don and Barb, the letter felt more like a long self-defense from the teacher, asserting her persistent and successful efforts to address Elaine's needs and to stay very "in tune" with Elaine's feelings. "I was both disappointed and surprised by Barb's comment that Elaine does not feel comfortable with me because she doesn't think I understand when she is feeling upset or confused."

Much of her letter simply missed the point, addressing issues only tangential to Elaine's struggles with aphasia and her anxieties surrounding her studies.

Expressing some understanding of Elaine's distress over the departure of Terri Ortlund, the teacher nonetheless suggested that Elaine "needs to see that many people can become special to her." Furthermore, she did not understand why the Schultzes had, at the suggestion of Dr. Levesque, held Elaine out of classes on that Thursday and Friday of the week after her shut down. She expressed "concern about the decreasing number of opportunities Elaine has for interacting with her peers" and said "we look for ways to increase the number of activities" with small groups. This teacher and some others had clung tenaciously to the conviction that Elaine merely needed more socialization.

The teacher insinuated that the problem lay more with Elaine than with her own teaching methods. "As a teacher, I think it is important to recognize that all learning situations are not the same. When students have difficulty with lessons, it is important to try different strategies and techniques."

Don, Barb, Sandi McGuire, Terri Ortlund, Annette McCormick,

Mrs. Chambers, and numerous other professionals agreed with that sentiment as a matter of principle. What baffled the Schultzes and their allies was the stubborn inflexibility that this and other teachers had in fact shown in their pedagogy.

The teacher also seemed badly out of touch with Elaine emotionally. "I saw some ups and downs during those days [following Elaine's traumatic shutdown], but nothing to indicate serious stress or consistent unhappiness," she said, in stark contrast to Sandi McGuire's comment, "I thought we were losing her." Instead of registering empathy for Elaine, the teacher wrote in defense of herself and her colleagues: "I firmly believe that all of the staff at Montana City School have worked very hard to accommodate the needs of your daughter."

That last claim especially rankled the Schultzes, after confronting such intractable resistance among MCS teachers and administrators. MCS personnel had consistently refused to change their teaching methods or engage in a credible effort to understand and respond properly to Elaine's aphasia. That such pleadings and defenses came so late, only after the Schultz's legal challenges and their announcement of Elaine's departure from MCS, rankled Don and Barb even more.

Elaine's other classroom teacher sent a second letter on January 13. Her distress over Elaine's absence sounded genuine to Don and Barb, and yet her letter also came late and felt vaguely defensive and accusatory. She insisted that she had always worked hard to do what was best for Elaine.

> I am still struggling with Elaine's absence from our daily life at school. I guess the way in which you chose to withdraw her from school left me with a feeling of emptiness…I have had to deal with the children's feelings of loss and their feelings of sadness when Elaine left so suddenly.

Barb and Don appreciated the sadness and frustration that the teacher conveyed. They also felt exasperated. Had they not said enough in IEP meetings, letters, or consults with teachers and administrators?

Had doctors, tutors, therapists, an attorney, and various teachers not sent clear and numerous appeals?

Don and Barb both understood the sense of disappointment and frustration felt among Elaine's teachers, but they felt stymied and exhausted. In early March of 1998, Barb wrote a letter to Dr. McCormick, explaining the decision they had finally made.

> On December 19, 1997, the decision to homeschool Elaine was made. In our hearts, we feel that we did everything possible to try and work with the Montana City School. The toll on Elaine, however, was too much, and both Don and I felt that we could not allow the shutdowns to continue, for the shutdown that occurred in December was profound.

Elaine, Barb, and Don were exhausted. Elaine's mental and physical health seemed precarious. They could not make satisfactory progress in a situation that had only regressed in four years. They were done.

CHAPTER 18

A Bright Direction

A Bold, Painful Decision

In her final communication, Superintendent Willett informed the Schultzes that, if they believed the school had failed to provide FAPE, they could file an official grievance. If they chose to do so, the state would assign a hearing officer to their case. They could also file for reimbursement of any paid services that, in their view, the school should have provided free of charge. On the other hand, she took a defensive position regarding any future interactions between the Schultzes and the school district: "Federal law states that no private school child with a disability has an individual right to receive some or all of the special education and related services" provided to public school students. Willett had understood the law correctly on all three points.

Considering Elaine's emotional health, her need to continue her education on pace, and the prospect of long, exhausting legal proceedings, Don and Barb changed course. They wrote a brief letter, dated January 1, 1998. "This is to inform you that we, Don and Barb Schultz, the parents of Elaine Schultz, will be homeschooling her beginning January 5, 1998." They also affirmed their intention to meet state educational regulations in their homeschooling of Elaine.

We will maintain accurate attendance records. We will document all materials and texts used in the educational process of our daughter. A portfolio containing samples of projects, papers, and tests will also be kept. We are aware that Elaine must have 180 days of instruction per fiscal year and will make certain that this requirement is met.

After years of exhausting effort, contention, and failed hopes, Elaine needed a drastic change. The Schultzes needed a new plan, even if a bold, somewhat risky plan. Despite their exhaustion and the anticipated rigors of homeschooling, they knew that delivering a full education to Elaine could and must happen.

They believed in Elaine.

Don and Barb Open a Homeschool

On January 5, 1998, Don and Barb officially opened their homeschool. Barb served as teacher, with two students, Elaine and her younger sister, Anna. In a letter on March 2 to Dr. McCormick, the Schultzes explained, "We named our school D & B Smith-Schultz School…In two months we have seen wonderful changes in Elaine. Her psychological demeanor has much improved, and we no longer see the problems she had while in public school."

In a similar letter to Dr. Jack Duffy, they detail the work that Barb had done so far and confirm the early positive results.

Asked why they did not begin homeschooling sooner, Barb recalls her desire to work part time. Homeschooling requires a very substantial time commitment. Furthermore, current opinion among neuropsychologists did not support homeschooling as a healthy option for a student. Withdrawal from regular social contact at school was contrary to children's developmental needs. On the other hand, every medical professional working with Elaine, her psychologist, pediatric neurologist, pediatricians, and therapists began urging Don and Barb to pull Elaine out of the public school system.

Through December of 1997 into January of 1998, Barb began an exhaustive process of starting over in preparation for homeschool with Elaine and Anna. On paper, both in words and imagery, "I drew a wall of blocks," she explains, "with all the pieces that Elaine had mastered, then determining the gaps in learning, no matter how elementary." This allowed Barb systematically to address each missing piece of knowledge and skill.

Barb relied heavily on visual instruction for language development, careful pacing, thoughtful repetition, and persistent encouragement.

Elaine continued her work with tutors at Sylvan for math and reading skills, with Alexis Flynn at St. Peter's Hospital for speech therapy, and with Sandi McGuire. Elaine and Anna enrolled together in an art course at the Holter Museum.

For both doctors, Barb and Don wanted to send an update in appreciation for their help and as affirmation and celebration of Elaine's progress. Elaine was learning now at a strong pace, with noteworthy joy and comfort. In an email to her sister on January 10, Barb said, "Already we are seeing a different child. Elaine is so much more relaxed, even cleaning her room without being asked." She loved learning, excelling in vocabulary and spelling. With past, relentless misemphasis on socialization in mind, Barb added a reassuring note: "Both Anna and Elaine have a girlfriend at the house to spend the night, and it is loud!!!!!!!!!!!!!!!!"

Freedom

Elaine says now, and emphatically, that the change from public school to homeschool was good for her. Finally, she could learn in an environment free of fragmented days, confusing expectations, conflicting voices, and the clamor of the classroom. She recalls the transition to homeschooling as a time of healing.

Even then, midway through her fourth grade year, Elaine embraced the idea of leaving MCS. "*When my mom and dad told me I would have school at home, I was like, 'Yeah! I'm okay with that!'"* Exasperated and out of patience with school officials, Don and Barb pulled Elaine's younger sister Anna out of MCS as well. Anna protested, never settling comfortably with the idea of homeschooling or being isolated from so many of her friends. The change did not work out well for her, so they returned Anna to MCS the following year, despite their ambivalence toward the school. For Elaine, however, the move was critically important and right.

Sandi McGuire delights in telling a story from a few years later, when Elaine was eleven years old. During a celebration called "Night to Shine" for students from Helena area schools, Sandi, Barb, and Don sat together through the student performances. Near the end, all the kids came out at once, from the front and back, spreading out and dancing down the aisles. Elaine stood aside at first, keeping to the shadows. Suddenly, her sister Anna grabbed her arm and pulled her into the dance. Elaine immediately loosened up and immersed herself in the occasion. "The two girls really got into it," recalls Sandi. "They had a ball."

Seeing Elaine become so free and joyful has remained a powerfully meaningful experience for Don and Barb, an affirmation of the confidence they felt in her from the beginning.

CHAPTER 19

Toward a Stronger Self

Signal Points on a New Path

With Elaine's move from public school to homeschool the long fight had finally ended. While Elaine embraced the move without hesitation, Don and Barb struggled with ambivalence—feelings of defeat, relief, frustration, exhaustion, and hope inextricably woven together with concern for Elaine's future. They felt no lack of confidence in Elaine's or Anna's abilities, and Barb had long since established confidence in her own teaching skills. Nonetheless, launching D & B Smith-Schultz School presented a daunting challenge. They met the challenge bravely, as did Elaine. From the second semester of her fourth grade year through age seventeen, Elaine progressed in her academic work and in her personal growth. A clearer, stronger identity emerged in Elaine through the years following her departure from public school.

Some of Elaine's most cherished recollections involve events that were unexceptional yet revealing of attitudes and abilities that had helped hold her together through her earlier trials.

Elaine enjoyed a deep and formative friendship with her maternal grandfather throughout her childhood. Over time, she had learned to mimic her grandpa's bold manner of speaking, reminiscent of his time in the navy. Barb recalls one comical incident on a family trip to Washington D.C. that reminded her and Don of how influential Elaine's grandpa had become. Having grown road weary, Elaine punctuated a long quiet spell with, "*My ass is tired. I need to stop!*" Taken aback, Don and Barb began to remonstrate with her, but sighed, rolled their eyes, and backed off. Elaine's grandfather, sitting in the back seat between the girls, was chuckling. Elaine says now, "*I was no Chatty Kathy, but I had gained a lot of confidence in my speech. I guess it showed in some comical ways now and then.*"

On the same trip, the family boarded a paddleboat in Nashville for a ride on the Mississippi River and followed that with a Tennessee Williams show at the Grand Ole Opry. Elaine remembers most clearly, and cherishes, an incident at the Opry involving another family. She learned travel directions quickly and gave directions adroitly. "*I was like a GPS at that age,*" she says (Barb insists that Elaine still is). Overhearing another family discussing confusedly how to navigate out of the Opry and then to their hotel, Elaine stepped in and offered them detailed directions.

> *I told them something like, "Go through those doors and down that hall, then take a right into the lobby and go out through the main entrance to the parking lot. Get on Opryland Drive and follow it north alongside Briley Parkway," and so on. I don't think they believed me at first. I was obviously really young.*

Elaine's confidence, along with reassurances from Don, Barb, and her grandpa, seemed to persuade them, and they gathered their luggage and headed through the doors and down the hall where Elaine had directed them. Her directions, in fact, were detailed, precise, and correct.

Learning to Be Elaine

As the next few years passed, Elaine's confidence in her ability to communicate grew, but the insecurities and confusions so common to early teenagers emerged as well. By age fourteen, Elaine was tired of other girls' fixation on being pretty. "*It annoyed me that they were always fussing over hairstyles, clothes, shoes, makeup, and body shape. I just didn't care."* She grew weary indeed of the relentless pressure they placed on each other and on her to look just this way or that. She rebelled. *"I entered my second 'boy phase',"* she recalls. While being "different" had contributed considerable pain to her earlier childhood, she nonetheless decided to defy the expectations of her peers. She dressed like a boy and cut her hair like a boy.

Elaine's defiance manifested more deeply, however, than she knew. In her effort to look more like the boys, Elaine curtailed her eating and became anorexic. Don, Barb, her therapist friend Sandi McGuire, and her doctor John Reynolds all grew concerned. Elaine was becoming not merely slim but alarmingly skinny. For several months, she refused to eat healthy portions at meals and denied being hungry. Sandi, Don, and Barb realized that this was a crisis point in Elaine's personal journey. She needed to find a way forward.

Elaine's relationship with Sandi McGuire was still strong, so the two of them worked effectively together, helping Elaine sort out her thoughts, feelings, and needs. Sandi communicated regularly with Don and Barb as well. They also had some sorting out to do. On the one hand, they knew that Elaine needed help, but they also realized on the other that her struggles toward independence were natural and necessary. They understood that her fight for greater autonomy needed to become explicit, fully conscious, and deliberate.

Parenting 102, a Crash Course

While pondering and praying over how to help Elaine through the next momentous stage in her life, Barb wrestled with her own painful self-revelation. She had long aspired to be a teacher, and an opportunity to attend seminary appealed strongly to her. "I took a course in seminary," she recalls. "A personal takeaway for me was that I had taken Elaine's voice from her and that doing so was sinful, as she was very capable. I had to repent of that. I had to let her advocate for herself. I gave her back her voice and allowed her to navigate. I feel she did a beautiful job."

Barb's understanding of how best to teach Elaine had taken an unexpected but critically important turn. Her role was to facilitate, guide gently, and encourage. She and Don did not have a plan, exactly, but an intention and a hope.

Like all parents, they found the way forward to be more difficult than they anticipated. "We knew already that Elaine as a small child was no clinging vine," says Barb, with a mildly ironic laugh, "but she decided she wasn't going to learn from us anymore." Indeed, Elaine had long since demonstrated both a desire and a capacity for asserting herself and standing up for herself. She was tough.

Elaine knew how to fight for her sense of self and dignity, but, like many teenagers, Elaine engaged the new battle with something less than perfect grace and forethought. *"The phase I was in during junior high was boredom and rebellion. My parents and teachers told me that I needed to begin advocating for myself, so I took their advice, maybe to an extreme."*

Barb and Elaine both laugh now at the irony of how fully and determinedly she began this new phase of self-advocacy.

Barb, Sandi, and others had always advocated for me, so I decided that I didn't need their help anymore. I began pushing everyone away so that I could speak for myself and take over. I didn't have a plan, but I thought maybe I should just keep doing things on my own, asking my own questions, and not depending on my mother at all. I knew that I couldn't make excuses for myself anymore. It was time to start talking with my own voice.

On the one hand, Elaine says, *"I began to communicate more. Communicating actually became easier. I had more confidence."* On the other hand, she recalls, *"Part of the reason I rebelled was that I still felt confused, and I needed to figure out who I was."* Thus, Elaine continued her fitful progress, like every teenager, through those formative years of ironic confidence and confusion.

Another Signal Point

Elaine learned to drive. She did not want to, but Don insisted. "You are fifteen years old. It is time," he said. In fact, Don *made* her learn to drive. She enrolled in a driver's ed class at the high school, and her instruction began. The county sheriff was her first classroom instructor, but only for the first day. In his brief presentation, he stressed the importance of learning and following the rules of the road, frightened the students with graphic images and harrowing scenarios, then completed his role as instructor by discussing how to handle a car in crisis situations. "*He was really nice,*" Elaine remembers, "*but he clearly thought I was a boy. I had really short hair, and I only wore jeans and a t-shirt. I didn't see any reason to set him straight.*"

The regular instructor stepped in on the second day. Unlike the sheriff, he seemed not to like the students, with the exception of the one boy in class, who apparently knew how to drive well from his experience growing up on a ranch. He also recognized that Elaine was, indeed, a girl.

The instructor seemed angry all the time, red-faced, impatient, and unkind. He spoke brusquely and belittled the students for making mistakes. As far as Elaine and her parents knew, he did not know that Elaine had aphasia, but he did accuse her in particular of wasting his time. According to the other students, that was the one thing he never said to anyone else. Elaine remembers one incident when she pushed passed feeling terrified of him. He had harshly insulted another student, and when the girl began to cry, Elaine spoke up in her defense. "*I guess that never changed about me,*" she says. "*No matter how afraid I was, I would defend someone being picked on.*"

The driving practice sessions felt nerve-wracking for Elaine. She understood the instructor's verbal instructions well enough, but she did not always perform well. "*I was really bad at parking and at slowing down to the speed limit on the highway. In town, it seemed like the teacher deliberately put me in the most difficult situations at all the 'malfunction junctions' in Helena. The other students said he did that to them too.*"

Despite her sometimes poor performances on the road, Elaine passed all the exams. At the end of the course, she gave the instructor a gift card to Ace Hardware. "*He acted surprised but clearly had no idea how to respond,*" she says, "*I don't remember him even saying 'Thank you'.*"

Smoother, Rougher, Forward

Elaine continued her academic progress and even excelled, both at home in the family D & B Smith-Schultz School and at the Sylvan Learning Center. Near the end of Elaine's high school sophomore year, Elisa Gauthier, a Sylvan teacher and instructor at Helena College, called Barb and said, "El is ready for some college level learning. She could easily pass my college course." In fact, says Elaine, "*I was really getting bored with what I was learning day in and day out. I wanted something more challenging.*" Mrs. Gautheir and Elaine's other Sylvan tutors decided to work with Barb to enroll Elaine in some courses at Helena College and, the following year, at Carroll College as well.

Apart from her academic coursework, Elaine took piano and ballet lessons and played on a recreational soccer team. She played the piano well, but as always, learned differently than most other students. She did not learn to read the music but memorized the motions of her hands and fingers and the layout of the piano keys. The same principle applied to her performance in ballet and soccer. "*Verbal instructions were not very helpful, even if I understood the words. I just pictured every move in my mind and practiced and memorized what I saw.*"

Elaine's profile as a student had not changed fundamentally, but late in her seventeenth year, she confronted the need for a different sort of learning. Among people with aphasia, difficulties with producing and processing language lead to heightened frustrations in personal relationships, loss of self-esteem, and reluctance to speak out. Living with aphasia very often involves feelings of isolation, even within the family. Because of such frustrations, people with aphasia are more vulnerable to abuse, exploitation, and manipulation. We define ourselves in part with language, assert ourselves with language, and defend ourselves with language. Elaine's challenges with language contributed to one of her most painful and humiliating experiences.

Elaine speaks confidently now about that experience, but the emotional difficulty remains. She met Derek, a young man about her age, online through a mass multiplayer online (MMO) gaming app. They connected through chats outside of the game as well, where they seemed to bond over personal issues. He was very talkative, friendly, endearingly supportive, and always ready with compliments. "*He really buttered me up*," Elaine says. "*We shared family stories and seemed to have so much in common as adopted children.*" Elaine began to feel very close to him. She had never allowed such a relationship before. "*I was so inexperienced*," she says, "*just really naive.*"

Derek expressed frequent and intense frustrations with his adoptive family, and while Elaine did not share the same negative feelings about her own family, his frustrations surrounding communication with his family resonated with her. She understood him; he understood her. That mutual understanding spoke deeply to Elaine's long-standing feelings of being alone and different. Derek's seeming ability to understand Elaine and his ease with her, despite her occasional struggles with articulating her thoughts and feelings, led Elaine to feel both comfortable and safe.

Not long after they met online, Derek came to visit Elaine and her family. They enjoyed their time together, and Don and Barb, feeling cautious and too much out of the loop, nonetheless found Derek to be pleasant and likeable. After he left, he and Elaine continued their online communication, with greater frequency and intensity. Don and Barb did not feel fully at ease with Elaine's choice, but they felt somewhat better after meeting Derek. Their confidence in Elaine would soon suffer a reversal.

Without informing Barb or Don, Elaine and Derek got engaged. Derek suddenly and dramatically changed. Before their engagement, he had always politely asked Elaine for help with his homework. Now he demanded it. "*He would not stop harassing me by email and phone*," Elaine says. If she refused or hesitated to help him as much as he wanted, he became mean and sarcastic. Elaine confesses that soon, she "*was really just doing his homework for him.*" He became routinely more verbally abusive and manipulative, often yelling angrily over the phone, demanding to know where she was and what she was doing.

Elaine remembers one exchange with Derek that awakened in her a deep sense of alarm. "*I forgot to tell him that I loved him, and he called me again and yelled at me.*" By that time, he had been calling and texting her multiple times every day. "*He was relentless,*" she says. "*Then he began talking to me about sex, telling me stories, hinting about what he wanted. That really made me uncomfortable.*" He began sending sexually explicitly pictures, and Elaine realized that he was deeply into pornography. "*He even wanted to video record me, but I said no way, I never wanted that.*" Again and again, he responded angrily and abusively.

Elaine no longer felt comfortable or safe in the relationship, but she wanted to work it out on her own, rather than depend upon her parents. "*Just like during my rebellious stage, I had decided that I could prove everyone wrong, even though I didn't know what I was trying to prove. In that relationship, I ended up being a big mess.*"

Under such emotional stress, however, Elaine found it especially difficult to communicate her feelings. How could she find the words to answer Derek, fluent and articulate even in his anger? And how could she find the words to tell her parents what was happening?

Don and Barb had not been comfortable with the relationship, but neither did they want to impose themselves. Over time, however, they grew more and more concerned, seeing Elaine growing highly stressed and deeply troubled. They began asking questions. Elaine revealed some, but not all, of what was happening, though enough for them to intervene. By this time, Elaine was open to their help. She let Barb and Don know that Derek wanted to attend her Helena College graduation, and Don stepped in with a resolute "No!"

Elaine felt relieved. She did not want Derek to attend and did not want to see him again. In response, Derek sent a long, abusive email to Don and Barb. He accused Barb of being "controlling" and disrespectful of the fact that he and Elaine were adults. Elaine had asked him not to send the email, but once again, he turned abusive. "You sound like your mother!" he would yell over the phone, among other insults and accusations that pitted her against her parents. And once again, she gave in to his verbose insistences and "arguments," and gave him permission to send it.

The email hurt Elaine, Don, and Barb deeply, leading to some angry exchanges and straining their own relationship. They all agreed, however, that Elaine needed to end the relationship. After nearly four years, at age twenty-one, Elaine severed her engagement and broke up with Derek. The relationship had done considerable damage, and Elaine's healing came slowly.

The painful time of introspection that followed proved fruitful for Elaine. Barb recalls, "I think that is when you began developing a new sense of identity. At first, you felt nothing. You had no feelings. None." Elaine agrees. "*Yes! I became a robot at first.*" Barb reminds Elaine that she made a decision on her own to talk to someone.

> *I felt alone. I needed help. I knew that. I had known that for a long time, but I was too proud to ask. I finally did. Mary Grace-Black, my counselor at HCC, helped me a lot. She put a lot of things in perspective for me. I don't know if I could thank her enough for that. I had no one else to talk to about it. I trusted her. I just needed to be away from everybody.*

Elaine's aphasia had contributed to her vulnerability in her relationship with Derek, as she struggled to represent herself adequately with words. In seeking help, she confronted the same dilemma.

> *No matter who I went to, I just sounded like my ex or like my family. I didn't know who I was either way. I obviously didn't know how to think for myself. It wasn't working any more, and I was alone and*

confused while I was going through it. I didn't even know what my dreams were yet. I only knew what I would say in third person.

Elaine shares a poignantly ambivalent bit of wisdom about her emotional state during her relationship with Derek. "*I stopped being myself. That was the biggest mistake of my life. But of course, if you don't know yourself, then how can you be yourself?*"

A Loss Before a Loss

On July 3, 2009, just two days after Elaine turned twenty-one, her beloved grandfather died. Perhaps with his passing, an integral part of Elaine's sense of self and security passed as well. Having been deeply uncomfortable in her relationship with Derek for a long time, she now felt even more alone and vulnerable without her grandfather. She broke up with Derek just a few weeks after her grandfather died and then focused her attention entirely on the loss of her dearest friend.

Grandpa had been like another father figure. He didn't worry about me. He knew I would make mistakes, but he knew I wouldn't run off and do stupid things. I do wish I had asked him more questions. I did ask him a lot of questions about his time in the Vietnam War. He talked to me a lot about that. He always told me that war was so ugly. No one really won. He lost a lot of friends there. I didn't mind him telling me about that, but I couldn't really imagine losing someone I loved like that. He saw so many people die in horrible ways, and he thought we weren't really helping the Vietnamese people. He stayed his cheery self though. I knew it took him many years to reach that point of mature peace.

Elaine was the only person he ever talked to about his experiences in the war, according to Barb. "She was the only one he would open up to. He saw her intelligence and her wisdom even at her age. He told me once that she would someday hold the family together."

Barb remembers too that Elaine's grandpa had dreamed of seeing Elaine succeed. He and Barb both had especially wanted her to be a Carroll College graduate. Elaine laughs about that. "*I never knew that until after he died. I only knew that you had that hope for me.*"

Elaine's role in her grandpa's funeral stands as another definitive point in her personal growth, especially her development of a stronger sense of self. "Elaine gave a wonderful speech at her grandpa's funeral. A lot of people were there," recalls Barb. "It was hard for her, but she did a beautiful job." Elaine nods her head and says,

> *That was my first speech ever. Knowing what to say was easy because it was personal, but it was also hard. It's not easy saying goodbye to someone you care about that much. It's not easy for me to express those kinds of feelings. I didn't focus on anyone listening. I just wanted to talk about him, what he did for me. I think that is why the nerves were not there, even though I was an emotional car wreck.*

The process of composing her memories and her feelings into words, words spoken in front of so many people, helped to settle some old and troublesome questions for Elaine: "*Can I speak well? Can I make sense? Can people understand me? Do I have a voice?*"

Mourning and Healing

Elaine needed time to heal, nonetheless. Losing her grandfather and severing her relationship with Derek, the two losses happening in so short a time, left Elaine feeling empty and weak. She and Barb often talk about the question of when Elaine finally settled into her adult identity. Elaine explains, adamantly,

> *Not until my mid-twenties. Definitely not right after my breakup! I needed to mourn that and mourn grandpa's passing. For a whole year, I was just a useless log. I couldn't go back and change anything.*

I don't recall if this was at twenty-four or twenty-five. It helped to go to the Episcopal Church at the time. It helped me figure out who I really was. That was hard, actually, after learning about church history—like a history of human failure and forgiving. I learned that no matter whom you go to, no one is perfect. That was a wake-up call. I realized how human everyone is. I was just starting to understand who I really was between twenty-four and twenty-six years old.

Elaine had begun to learn more deeply that she was, after all, not so different. As a woman with aphasia, with "differences," and personal failures and frustrations, she did not stand outside of society looking in. She was like others. Others were like her.

Another important step in Elaine's journey toward healing, self-understanding, and self-confidence came with her first job at age twenty-four. She interviewed for and was hired as a technician at a molecular lab in St. Peter's hospital. Despite some early confusions and tensions, she kept the job for over a year and found the work rewarding. In fact, her hiring had involved some odd misunderstandings about the specific courses she had taken at Helena College and at Carroll College. Her supervisor thought she had substantial preparation in chemistry, while her course work involved computer tech primarily.

The tasks initially assigned to her did not fit her abilities, so her supervisor reassigned Elaine to computer data entry, site maintenance, and some programming. That change led to a revelation for Elaine:

As a teenager, I didn't think I was smart enough. I didn't have that kind of self-confidence; so, I didn't believe what anyone told me about my abilities. I didn't realize again until my first job that I still had passion for computers. I loved working with them I was good at it.

She earned consistent praise among her co-workers for her work with the lab computers, reigniting her love for such work. Sitting at the data entry desk every day, she realized that she could pursue studies in computer technology and employ her skills professionally.

CHAPTER 20

A Steady Walk

Today, and Ready for Tomorrow

Now in her early thirties, Elaine has a strong sense of self. Her most recent history brought new challenges, but, knowing her limitations and her capabilities, she met them with a quiet determination and confidence. In her late twenties and on until age thirty-one, Elaine carried the role of primary care giver for both of her grandmothers. Her mother provided steady help most of the time, but her own persistent health issues sidelined her now and then, while the grandmother's needs routinely complicated Elaine's schedule at home, at work, and at school. Elaine managed her complex life well—the emotional stresses, the logistics and the multifaceted communication with college faculty and staff, and with parents and grandmothers.

Elaine's life has very recently grown a bit simpler, but at a personal cost. Elaine's paternal grandmother moved away and now lives with Don's brother, and more recently her maternal grandmother passed away. Elaine and Barb (and I) are at work now on the grandmother's obituary. Once again, Elaine finds herself working on questions of what to say and how to say it best.

Assuming that all goes as planned, Elaine will graduate from Carroll College with a bachelor's degree in computer engineering after the fall semester of 2022. Her progress through college has been slow by choice, but steady and marked by success. A relationship with a new boyfriend feels safe, comfortable, encouraging, and steady. Her computer maintenance and data-entry work with her dad's business satisfies her for now. To questions about what she will do next, Elaine responds with a shrug, an easy smile, and says, "Who knows?"

Some Final Notes

Elaine will always live with aphasia. She will live, therefore, with the question of what her aphasia will mean for her through all the same kinds of life experiences that we all have. What we know is that her aphasia will not set her apart unless others thoughtlessly insist that it does. What we know is that she is us; we are her. How do we realize that for ourselves? For the many Elaines among us? First, we avoid the facile "we-they" formulations and the inevitable misunderstandings that follow.

Laboring under those divisive formulations, we assume our own normalcy and the adequacy of our own understanding. We do not, in other words, assume that we are also the ones who need to learn. And we build our world accordingly, excluding those who fall outside of our self-affirming definitions. The term "ableist" describes a society constructed by and for those we consider to be fully "able" (non-disabled). Our physical spaces assume an exclusive use by narrowly defined "able-bodied" people, just as our modes of communication (including our pedagogies) tend strongly to welcome only the non-disabled. Perhaps I can make the point with some mild hyperbole: Much of the disability they (the "disabled" community) face is merely the sum of obstacles that we place in their way. We live in an ableist society; therefore, we live in a society that discriminates by design.

It serves no one well to be dismissive of the challenges that people with disabilities, their parents, and their educators face together. For instance, educators face a three-fold challenge, on behalf of highly capable students who function differently than most and need other than the usual forms of help. First, educators must preserve their high academic performance standards. Second, they must rethink and revise their instructional methods. Third, they must also reconceive their notions of how students can adequately demonstrate mastery.

Most of Elaine's educators met those challenges with patience and creativity. Some expressed persistent frustration and distanced themselves. In that regard, Elaine's story mirrors the stories of students all over the country, in virtually every school and at every level of education. With varying levels of enthusiasm, acceptance, suspicion, or indifference, school administrators and teachers confront the need for creative thinking, for doing their jobs a little differently than they have before and for allowing some students to demonstrate their knowledge and skills in unique ways.

Students with disabilities have not set themselves apart by their successes; rather, their successes, matching those of non-disabled students, have placed them squarely and properly among the student population in general. They are us; we are them.

In school and virtually everywhere else, language is one of the most powerful means by which we define ourselves, others, and our world. We use language in order to connect with or separate from others and articulate our places in the world. Whatever other means of connecting that we may employ, we swim in a sea of words, day in and day out. People with aphasia, in varying degrees of severity, often feel disconnected from the rest of us, as if drowning in our verbal and textual sea.

Whatever difficulties with language that they may experience, whether mild, moderate, or severe, we cannot assume that they are out of reach. The world that we create through language will include them best when we learn to listen and adapt, turning our close attention to them and finding ways to build connections with them. The words we speak on their behalf matter greatly in the ongoing discussions and debates about how best to teach and communicate. The words we speak to them matter more. The words they speak to us matter most.

Epilogue from Elaine

Some Thoughts on Being Different, Being Supported, and Being Bold

At six years old, I painted my grandparents' house. It was my grandfather's turn to babysit, but he had fallen asleep. Actually, I mostly painted the kitchen. My grandma was an artist, so she had a lot of acrylic paints. I didn't touch her paintings or her painting tools, but I borrowed her paints. I remember how the paint felt in my hands, so I guess I was "finger painting." I got paint high up on the cupboards. I meant to paint all of the wood. It needed more color! I even painted one of the counters. I painted my sister Anna in the process, all over her body and face. I wanted everything to look colorful and pretty.

When my grandpa woke up, he was not happy. "What have you done?" he asked, with his voice raised. Anna and I could tell that Grandpa was upset, but we were not frightened. I knew I was in trouble, but Grandpa had already begun laughing so hard he was shaking, even as he tried to act a little angry. He picked us both up and put us straight into the bathtub. After we got done with our bath, Grandpa went out into the back yard where he could laugh out loud without us hearing him. He told me later that he laughed so hard he cried.

Grandma laughed about it eventually, but it took her a little longer. They both had to deal with a lot of acrylic paint dried all over the kitchen. They put us in "time out" afterwards, but they never left me or Anna feeling humiliated. As I look back on the experience now, I feel accepted and affirmed.

My path has been different than most, but I have become much more aware of how many people live with disability and face obstacles and difficulties similar to mine. I do still feel different. I still depend on visual cues, especially body language, more than most people seem to. At least I am very aware of and conscious of my need to interpret those kinds of cues deliberately. I often hear from people that they did not know I have any disability. It is more or less apparent, depending on the day, or how tired I am, or how distracted. When I get very tired or stressed, my speech sometimes gets a bit muddled. At my worst, I think I sound like I am drunk. My enunciation grows poor, and so does my grammar. I still experience some effects of the cerebral palsy, also, a weakness and lack of coordination on my left side. I am still a toe walker. I remind myself that I am a stroke survivor.

In my early teens, I didn't want to hear about my aphasia. I didn't want to be different in that way, but I didn't want to play the victim card for anyone's pity either. Pity is the worst sort of empathy. On the other hand, with a lot of self-contradiction, I pitied myself. I used my disability as an excuse for not trying to accomplish anything, but I refused to ask anyone for help. I just wanted to be "normal."

In my late teens, I set out to change my attitude. No more excuses. No more holding back. When I first enrolled in college-level classes at Helena College, my fear was huge. I had little confidence in myself being again in a public school environment. Two things were true, however. First, I was surprised at how many teachers and staff stepped in to help when I asked. Second, the more I pushed past my fears, the more I realized that it was not as bad as I feared. I began to appreciate more how helpful so many people had been before—my parents, teachers, tutors, doctors, and therapists. My mom and grandpa, especially, had been my Anne Sullivans.

Even now, I am realizing more deeply how important my grandma and grandpa were. My grandmother on my mother's side died recently. I miss her terribly. Like my grandfather, she always believed in me and told me often that she was proud of me. In fact, both of my grandmothers insisted that getting an education was essential for me. They let me know that I could make it through college.

Now, I self-teach a lot. I do not give up, no matter how difficult the task or embarrassing my mistakes. I ask for help when I need to. My love of math tells me something about myself. I tend to be pretty black and white, and a lot of math lends itself to black-and-white thinking—a problem has one correct answer, even if getting to the answer is a complex process. Not all math is like that, however, and calculus forced me to think differently. Calculus involves so much uncertainty. It terrified me at first, and I avoided it when I was younger. In college, with help from patient teachers, I finally mastered it.

I hope people with disabilities will read this book and feel encouraged to keep trying. If you fail, get up and try again. I know that aphasia is different from one person to the next. Not everyone with aphasia or other disabilities has the support I have had from teachers, therapists, doctors, advisors, parents, tutors, and friends. Yes, we all confront people, even professionals in fact, who want to push us away. I don't want this book to discourage anyone about academia, but I want people to be aware. You will always encounter people who do not understand or who are bullies, but believe in yourself and know that you will also find people who want to help.

I hope this book will also encourage non-disabled people to get involved and reflect on how people with disabilities live and interact in the world. We deeply appreciate the support we get. We now and then feel terrified by circumstances, but that is normal for everyone. Like everyone, we learn to manage. We each have our own distinct pace for learning and working; but we make our way very well.

www.ingramcontent.com/pod-product-compliance
Lightning Source LLC
Chambersburg PA
CBHW050256010526
44107CB00033B/1398/J